A Bridge of Stories

Risking It All to Connect Classrooms and Cultures in Belize

One Storyteller's Unexpected Journey

Students excited to share their work at Bishop Martin Roman Catholic School, grade four, in San Ignacio, Cayo District, Belize.

A Bridge of Stories

Risking It All to Connect Classrooms and Cultures in Belize

One Storyteller's Unexpected Journey

Kristin Pedemonti

Parkhurst Brothers Publishers
MARION, MICHIGAN

www.parkhurstbrothers.com

Parkhurst Brothers books are distributed to the trade through the Chicago Distribution Center, and may be ordered through Ingram Book Company, Baker & Taylor, Follett Library Resources and other book industry wholesalers. To order from Chicago Distribution Center, phone 1-800-621-2736 or send a fax to 800-621-8476. Copies of this and other Parkhurst Brothers Inc., Publishers titles are available to organizations and corporations for purchase in quantity by contacting Special Sales Department at our home office location, listed on our web site. Manuscript submission guidelines for this publishing company are available at our web site.

Printed in the United States of America   First Edition, 2017

2017 2018 2019 2020   12 11 10 9 8 7 6 5 4 3 2 1

Library of Congress Cataloging in Publication Data: [Pending]

ISBN: Trade Paperback 978-1-62491-087-6
ISBN: e-book 978-1-62491-088-3

Parkhurst Brothers Publishers believes that the free and open exchange of ideas is essential for the maintenance of our freedoms. We support the First Amendment of the United States Constitution and encourage all citizens to study all sides of public policy questions, making up their own minds. Closed minds cost a society dearly.

Cover and interior design by   Linda D. Parkhurst, Ph.D.
Proofread by   Parkhust Brothers Staff
Acquired for Parkhurst Brothers Inc., Publishers
and edited by: Ted Parkhurst

012017

Contents

Acknowledgements

Thank you to Neftali Lemus for the initial invitation and for trusting in my skillset more than I did. You opened a whole new world to me, for which I am eternally grateful.

Thank you to everyone in Belize who assisted with the project. Thank you for promoting this work, inviting me to your schools and libraries, and for collaborating with me. Thank you to Rose Bradley, Agnes Morris, Teacher Barbara, Nicole Eusey, Mrs. Shaw of St. Barnabas School, Librarian Terry Ulloa, Lucy at Belize National Library, Principal Najarro at Bishop Martin Roman Catholic School, the students at Bishop Roman Catholic School and Immaculate Conception in Bullet Tree Falls, the Belize National Teachers Union—especially to Elena Smith, the staff at Sacred Heart Junior College—especially Janeen Quiroz, Teacher Indira, Teacher Carla, and Principal Torres at St. Joseph Roman Catholic School in Belize City, Peace Corps volunteers Margaret Ellsworth, Anna Sommerhauser, and Ava Hacker, Theo Cocchi and Naida of the Parrot Nest—thank you for the support you offered by inviting me into the Nest and treating me like one of the family, the Williams family in Belize City—my first "second" family, and finally thank you posthumously to Matthew Klinck for all your generosity and kindness in filming and editing the teacher-training videos during January 2012.

I express deepest gratitude and appreciation for monetary support of this volunteer project especially to Allison Rotteveel, Belize City Rotary Club, Cathy L., David Claunch, Faith S., Gus, Indiegogo Campaign Contributors, Keen, the Kilroy Family, Layla Darwich, Marlborough Elementary School, Patti Klein, Robin Reichert, and Rosendo Urbina.

Thank you, Ted Parkhurst of Parkhurst Brothers Publishers, for trusting my readiness to write this book and for believing in me every time I protested the "doing."

Thank you, Elizabeth Ellis, for inspiration and encouragement.

Thank you to the storytellers who paved the way and inspired me to leap into this life: Bil Lepp, Bill Harley, Diane Edgecomb, Donald Davis, Elizabeth Ellis, Heather Forest, Jim May, Laura Simms, Margaret Read MacDonald, Karen Chace and Noa Baum.

Thank you to David Claunch for being one of the best cheerleaders in the universe. I appreciate every conversation, every bubble and every hug of encouragement you shared, as I worked my way through the writing of this book.

Thank you to Julie Moss for encouragement, excellent advice, and editing eyes on the first draft.

Thank you to Paul Andrew Smith for so generously gifting the MacBookPro upon which the first draft was completed. Thank you for edits and eyes on the second draft: Ad Booth, Amanda Baker, Csenge Zalka, Dawn Miller Carone, Mary Garrett, Stanislaus Ziolkowski, and Terri Mintz. Thank you Kyle Cardinal for continual encouragement during the editing process.

Thank you, again, to Robin Reichert, for traveling with me to Belize during the early stages of the project and then again for the last trip in January of 2012. Your ongoing support, heart, and soul mean so much to me. Thank you for guidance and gentle encouragement.

Thank you to cousin Alison Black for always supporting my dreams. Thank you to my family for accepting me for who I am and allowing me to pursue my dreams.

Introduction

Every culture has a story. Every person has a story. Stories serve many functions, one of which is to connect us one to another, build bridges between peoples, dispel stereotypes and illustrate our commonalities while honoring our diversity. Listening to and sharing stories is important because our communities are more diverse than ever.

Stories provide a sense of self and a sense of place within the world. Stories illustrate how the world is interconnected. Through story we see each other as individuals and as human beings, rather than as subjects of governments or restrained by man-made borders that sometimes seem to cause divisions. We also become aware of how similar we are. When our stories are valued, we feel valued. Reclaiming and honoring the wisdom of indigenous stories by offering a process to utilize them in classrooms and communities goes a step further to instill a deeper sense of value in these stories and reawaken the collective knowledge of the past by bringing it to the present. Stories connect across time: past to present, and present to future.

This book is a culmination of my experience working in the field for seven years. I approached this time with little background in pedagogy or anthropology. Possessing a deep passion for learning about cultures, I wanted to enhance understandings of indigenous and marginalized populations within their own country and beyond their own borders. I hoped to encourage respect and understanding between those cultures. My hope is that through learning more about their cultural stories and the valuable lessons therein, that the next generation of Belizeans will feel a sense of pride about who they are and the value that their stories hold. It is also my hope that those beyond Belizean borders will understand the value of these stories. These pages present:

> The evolution of the project.
> Challenges faced and overcome.
> A step-by-step guide to one creative writing exercise using indigenous culture in the classroom.
> A selection of students' and teachers' stories that were the result of the writing workshops presented.
> Helpful tips—based on my hundreds of hours in classrooms and in faculty workshops—that should be of value to anyone wishing to implement this or similar cultural-based writing exercises with K-12 populations in any country.

My goal in this book is to share the work with a broader audience and demonstrate how this program can be replicated anywhere anyone chooses.

The process applied here can be replicated worldwide and across a wide range of interests. I am sharing my experience which I hope may benefit educators, storytellers especially, but also others interested in learning what is involved in creating and facilitating a project in another country or community. If you find inspiration in my own journey, please feel free to employ the processes explained here in your own planning and implementation.

This book honors the inherent value of all indigenous stories. We desperately need to connect across cultural boundaries in order to foster greater understanding. Some may choose to use this book in their advocacy for similar work in other cultures. I hope the explanation of my experience and the process that developed during my work will enable research into stories and legends—both those of readers' native cultures and those of other cultures of interest. Finally, I hope that this work will encourage readers to learn from as many cultures as possible and to value the wisdom within each tradition.

The stories included were written by Belizean youth and teachers based on age-old Belizean legends shared in workshops. However, this book is more than simply stories collected and shared by an outsider who became accepted as an insider. The stories presented here were written by a doubly marginalized group: their voices are not heard first because of being indigenous and second because they are youth. Their voices need to be heard and encouraged so as to inspire the next generation of storytellers and story-writers. Educators in Belize have told me that this process had lasting value, both as those teachers who attended the workshops shared the creative writing lesson with other teachers and encouraging young Belizeans to tell and share their stories. Their wisdom needs and deserves to be recognized.

Not only do young indigenous people need to honor their native stories, but wider audiences are hungry to include their voices in the worldwide chorus of story traditions. In every educational setting, educators need a way to connect to an ever increasingly diverse student population. Chapter Three provides a plan to do just that—for teachers to connect to students and students to connect to each other through their stories.

Students also need and deserve an opportunity to connect fully with the lessons and material being taught. Regrettably, many educational systems have transformed into teaching to the test. Each year there is less opportunity for teachers to allow creative expression. Teachers are required to implement programs that largely exclude student's experience of their native culture, its rich history, and personal meaning in their lives. While there is undeniable value in teaching facts of science and the hard knowledge of math, detachment from students' cultural heritage works lasting effects upon the growing psyche.

However, it is that cultural exploration and creative expression which gives students an opportunity to truly connect to the lessons and to become fully engaged in the material. Students have to see themselves in the lessons being taught. They shine when they see themselves and connect. Not only must they see themselves in their study, but we need to help them find connections to each other, neighbors, and communities. That happens when the curriculum engages their values, their heritage, and their destiny. Stories address so many growth issues and provide a dynamic step to that connection. My hope is that you will find within these pages some inspiration and a lesson plan that excites you, whether in classroom or community.

↬

A Typical Day in the Life of the Project:

> ➤ 6 am Wake up. Coffee or tea with fruit or oatmeal, prepare for the day in my ten foot by ten foot room.
> ➤ 8 am Walk to a local school, anywhere from one to three miles, or take the bus to a local village.
> ➤ 9 am Arrive at school and ask to speak to the principal, librarian or head teacher.
> ➤ 10 am to 11:30 am Often within the same day, visit classrooms and offer read-alouds.
> ➤ 11:30 am to 1 pm Most schools took ninety minute breaks because many students walked home for lunch with their families.
> ➤ 1:15 pm to 3:30 pm Offer read-alouds or a workshop for one class or grade level and schedule follow-up meetings for the next day or the next.
> ➤ 3:30 pm Walk home or bus home. Take a one-hour siesta.

As the program evolved over time, my afternoons/evenings looked like this:

> ➤ 4:30 pm to 9:30 pm or later: Edit work submitted by students in workshops.

Expansion:

From September 2005 to February 2012, success in one school or library or village led to scheduling requests from another school or library in a nearby village. Everywhere I traveled, I met more teachers, librarians, or principals who would invite me to come to their school or library to offer a program and collaborate on a project. Somehow, as fate would have it,

I connected with the Belize National Teacher's Union. At that time, the president of the union responded to my work and gave me a platform to promote teacher workshops as well as school visits sharing and modeling the program. Workshops were usually held in schools or libraries and attendance varied from nine to eighty. A typical half-day workshop took place on Saturdays. Educators would come from the local village school and often other teachers would join from nearby villages as well. The workshop space was often a classroom in a concrete block school in which sound reverberated off the walls, large ceiling fans whirred overhead, (when there was electricity) chickens clucked outside, and one could sometimes see students gathered in the courtyard; boys playing with a soccer ball, girls gathered in conversation. Our "technology" consisted of a blackboard and chalk—and teachers took notes with paper and pens. Though we may have lacked for modern technology, we made up for it in creativity. More on that later as the story unfolds.

Before I knew it, I'd gone on a grand adventure visiting over seventy-five villages, one hundred schools, and twenty libraries throughout the country, donating programs for over thirty-three thousand students and training eight hundred teachers to use their own cultural stories in the classroom. The project evolved beyond my wildest expectations. What I thought I was going to do transformed into something else entirely. I thought I might visit a dozen or so schools, donate a few hundred books, train a few dozen teachers and hopefully inspire a hand full of students and teachers to see the value in storytelling, whether their own cultural legends or in the specific books shared.

Disclaimer and a Few Notes:

One Woman's Experience and How it Might Serve You

I hope my experience in creating this project, listening, learning, developing relationships with locals, and overcoming some specific challenges will in some way serve you as you may seek to create your own project or program.

I ask you, the reader, to remember that this is one woman's experience of creating and facilitating a volunteer project in another culture. This is my personal experience of what happened. Of course, it is one person's perception. My experience developed from starting a project out of passion and a deep connection to the people and their culture; a relationship that developed over time. The program did not come from the world of academia, nor from an initial thought of impacting or changing an educational system. I had no idea how far the project would go. The process was literally one student, one teacher, one librarian, one school, one village at a time.

I had no plan for which schools or which villages I traveled to first. I simply travelled to and shared lessons with whoever requested me to come. There was no over-arching plan. My work developed according to what locals asked and where they sent me. I am honored by their trust in me. I believe that part of the reason the project has been so successful is because I did not come in with outside ideas or an agenda. I arrived a clean slate, open to doing my best to provide what was asked.

I had no idea that this project would eventually evolve into a book. For this, I am deeply grateful. This book presents the evolution and template for a project that was successful in Belize. It includes the stories that resulted from workshops presented. My hope is that the project can be replicated elsewhere. I have used the same writing exercise in inner city and rural schools in the United States, in Ghana and in France with the same result: students and teachers became deeply engaged in the use of their stories in the classroom. I have also been invited to Nepal post-earthquake to share a version of this project in late 2016.

Belizean Legend Structure:

Many Belizean legends do not follow traditional structure but are rather first-hand accounts of what people believe they experienced when encountering spirits. There is a deep respect in Belizean villages for various legends. There is a widespread belief that traditional legends are not simply stories. Most Belizeans believe these legends reveal actual beings or spirits. They believe that retelling the legends serves a deep purpose in providing important lessons. Interacting with and listening to the legends shared and gifted to me by the Belizean people, I learned deep respect for stories and legends from cultures other than my own.

CHAPTER ONE

How Belize Became My Second Home

A Little Belize Background:

If like me, you remember Belize vaguely as a footnote from your school days—or perhaps have never even heard of the country—here's a little background to give you some context.

Belize is a tiny country located beneath the Yucatan peninsula of Mexico and next to Guatemala. It is semi-tropical and has a long coast of Caribbean Sea as well as rich rain forest. The population is around three hundred thousand. The four most prominent cultures are Creole, Garifuna, Maya, and Mestizo. You will hear mostly Belizean Creole being spoken. It sounds very similar to English, but has western African syntax and is spoken rather rapidly. If you listen carefully you should understand. You will also hear music everywhere you go because music is part of life in Belize. So, whether you travel on a local bus or are walking down the street, you will hear punta rock, reggaeton, dance-hall and "souls."

Belize City, which became my second home, is home to about ninety thousand people doing their best to eek out a living. It is not much of a modern city. The roads are narrow, the Northern Highway is a two-lane road, and many of the roads within Belize City are so narrow I am not sure how two cars are able to pass each other at the same time. Most houses are small, from two to four rooms and made of concrete block or two-by-four wooden construction. Clustered very tightly together, the concrete block houses are often painted pale yellow or that green you may have seen in hospitals or schools. The wooden homes are not usually painted, just plain wood sometimes in various states of dilapidation. There are few embellishments on most houses, although there is a wealthy section of Belize City where the expats live. These neighborhoods—with their high, whitewashed concrete fences, elaborate iron gates, and security systems—stand in stark contrast to the rest of the city. Beyond the gates are manicured lawns, flowering shrubbery and ornately carved wooden doors. Though I often wondered how this contrast felt to my Belizean friends, I never dared to ask that question.

One thing I always noticed was the garbage. Few bins around the city meant that people simply tossed their garbage onto the streets or the narrow, chipped-concrete sidewalks. Once or twice a week you would see street cleaners, not the mechanical kind, but a group of men and women with wheelbarrows who would collect the detritus from the streets and sidewalks and wheel it to larger piles scattered throughout the city. There were no high-rises when I arrived in 2005. The tallest building was perhaps four stories. Belize is a hub for international banking.

The largest industry is tourism. In fact, twenty-five percent of the population works in tourism. There are no fast food chains—which I think is wonderful! Belizean fast food is served from small shacks on the roadsides where salbutes, empanadas, tacos, burritos, johnny cakes, powder buns, and some days special treats such as escabeche or tamales are offered.

The transportation system is comprised of old school buses brought down from the US and run by several different companies. Some of the buses remain yellow while others are painted white with orange trim or sky blue, the various colors of the several competing bus companies. Traveling within the city or village to village is quite cheap; anywhere from one dollar US for a one-hour journey to perhaps ten dollars US if you are traveling several hours. The buses run on a relatively regular basis, and the schedule was somewhat dependable. If you are friendly (like me) and join conversations on the buses, very soon you will be invited to share a pot of rice and beans or perhaps a glass of fresh watermelon juice. The roads are in various states of disrepair, kind of like they are in many US states. Street signs are not that different from what you might see in your own town or city. In Belize City, loads of billboards advertise everything from local cell phone companies to extolling the virtues of the local power company.

The Reality of my Life in Belize Compared to What My Friends Thought

Contrary to what some of my friends thought back home, I was not sipping mai tais on the beach. I lived in a ten foot by ten foot room made of concrete block, with a tin roof. I had a bed, a homemade wooden table, a chair, a fan and an indoor bathroom. On days when it was 110°F in my room, I was grateful for the fan and the electricity. I was not happy about the frequent blackouts! Even in the largest and most "modern" city, they happened on a regular basis. Sadie and Bulma, two huge Rottweilers, lived just outside my room on the concrete patio and watched out for me. The Williams family upstairs took great care of me. They quickly became a second family—often inviting me to join in for rice and beans for lunch or to sit on their veranda and enjoy the cool late afternoon breeze over a cup of fresh lime juice.

And soon Belize City became my second home. The day I knew I was "home" was when, walking home from presenting at St. Joseph's Roman Catholic School, I saw perhaps a dozen children leaning out the bus windows waving at me and calling out, "Story Lady, Story Lady, when you coming back? We love you, Story Lady!" Their enthusiasm encouraged me to continue pushing ahead, one story, one school at a time.

But first, like the song says, "Let's start at the very beginning/A very good place to start …"[1] and let me tell you how it all began.

Why Belize?

I did not choose Belize. Belize chose me. Before July of 2005, Belize was a footnote from my school days, though it was then known as British Honduras. I had no idea that visiting Belize on

---

1. "Do-Re-Mi", from *The Sound of Music*. Writer, Oscar Hammerstein II, composer Richard Rodgers, 1959.

a holiday would lead to a life-altering adventure.

The whole journey of this volunteer project—which I called Literacy Outreach Belize—and ultimately the writing of this book came together from an initial chance meeting with one person, Neftali Lemus, on a boat in the Caribbean Sea off the Belizean coast on July 5, 2005. Neftali was our Belizean snorkel instructor and guide. We had just finished a snorkel excursion, part of the adventure of the storytelling cruise with Bil Lepp. Neftali and I struck up a conversation. Like many, he had never met a professional storyteller before. He was intrigued by my career path, my experience as a children's librarian, ovarian cancer researcher, and performer. Indeed, I possess a deep passion for stories, for the process of connecting, and making a difference.

After hearing me express my passion, Neftali shared a grim reality: for a multitude of reasons, the literacy rates in Belize had plummeted over the last few decades. Although the official statistics indicate a seventy-five percent literacy rate—the latest statistics I could find from UNESCO were dated 1991—the reality of functional literacy is perhaps often closer to fifty percent. He was genuinely concerned about the opportunities, or lack thereof, for the next generation. Neftali expressed that he felt I possessed the skill set necessary to reach out to the children and teachers in his country and positively impact literacy. Now I was intrigued, especially given my interest in work that made a positive impact.

And so it began. That chance meeting on a boat led to two months of email exchanges with Neftali and ultimately an invitation to return to Belize on my birthday, September 3, 2005. The seed was planted for Literacy Outreach Belize to blossom. During that visit, I presented a poetry workshop at Muffles College in Orange Walk Town. That workshop focused on using the five senses to describe in detail where one is from and was based on George Ella Lyon's poem "Where I am From."[2] The program was received with enthusiasm. Showered with thanks by attendees, I witnessed first-hand the need for teacher training and literacy outreach. I returned home inspired.

Bit by bit, pieces came together so that the initial seed planted could blossom into a full-blown project. In my experience, there were several pieces already in place. July 1, 2005, my amicable divorce was finalized, we are still friends. August 1, 2005, I had left my job as children's librarian and head of youth services at Upper Perkiomen Valley Library in Red Hill, Pennsylvania to pursue full-time storytelling, performing at that time in schools and libraries across the state. The next leap seemed rational at the time. I decided to sell my home and use some of the proceeds to create a volunteer project, Literacy Outreach Belize. My home sold to the very first person who saw the for sale sign: a man with five children. This was truly amazing because I had sent up a prayer saying I wanted a family to live in this house and bloom. Now, here they were!

Caveat, the closing was in seventeen days! I needed to move very quickly! So my next step was obvious. I needed to sell or give away most of my possessions. Some of my possessions ended up with dear friends. The antique steamer trunk ended up at a high school chum's house. My secondhand—but still lovely—overstuffed couch, loveseat, armoire, the cobbled-together all-cherry

2. http://www.georgeellalyon.com/where.html

bedroom set with a beveled mirror was bought lock, stock, and barrel by Jupiter Jen, a performer I had met when I booked programs at the library.

My mother's house in Allentown, Pennsylvania, became my base of operations the first year as I traveled back and forth to Belize to lay the groundwork for the project. When in Belize, I visited schools asking to meet with principals and teachers. I described the skill set I possessed and then listened to their needs, their challenges and their desires. After all the listening and learning about how I could best assist, I did months of research to learn how to best serve the staff and schools. That process is described in more detail later in the chapter.

This entire process and experience has changed my life in ways I never imagined. Leaving a full-time job to become a full-time storyteller and then selling my home and most of my possessions paved the way for my later willingness to take other risks and seize opportunities such as auditioning and being accepted to perform in storytelling festivals in Colombia, Kenya, and Iran. It led to the courage to audition for TED Talks Talent Search and be selected as a finalist for the USA. It led to an interview at the World Bank where I now work as a storytelling consultant.

Truth be told, there was a romance, too. Remember Neftali Lemus, the young man who initially invited me to Belize and planted the seed for the project? We dated for nearly a year during that first phase of the project. Ironically, that romance ended a few months before I decided to move to Belize. However, we remain good friends to this day. The relationship with Belize, the indigenous cultures, and the legends had just begun.

Literacy Outreach Belize: Its Creation, the Journey and Evolution

Laying the Groundwork

First things first. From the get-go, I realized that—even before beginning a project of this magnitude, there are a few steps to take and things to consider.

So, how do you make the first connection? Find out which form of communication usually works best based on cultural norms. For example, do they prefer formally set up face-to-face meetings or email contact or a phone call introduction? Is it best for you to be introduced by someone locally: another teacher or a parent from the community? Do you need to interact first with a formal organization or government official such as the Ministry of Education? Are these channels truly necessary for your work to continue?

What do you wear? Be culturally sensitive. Make sure you have dressed appropriately. This may seem like simple common sense, but make sure you are not unintentionally causing offense by failing to honor cultural norms. For example, although it was perfectly acceptable to walk around the streets of Belize in shorts, t-shirt, and flip-flops, it was not okay to show up at a school to volunteer in that outfit. In Belizean schools and businesses, a woman must always wear at least cap-sleeves and either pants or a skirt that reaches the knee. It was never appropriate to wear a spaghetti-strap top. Flip-flops were usually frowned upon as well. Look professional, but don't go overboard; wearing an expensive outfit with lots of jewelry can be just as much of a potential barrier, unintentionally creating an air of superiority.

It is often most effective and efficient to show up in person at a school and ask to speak with either the principal, vice principal, or an enthused teacher. This is a small piece of advice I am sharing from my own journey. I discovered that I usually identified my best contact simply by observing their personality and interaction with the students on the school grounds. I would explain I was there to offer my services free of charge, for example, to read a few books aloud with their students. Together we decided if and when to share the activity.

I found out that official channels are often not necessary and can be counter-productive. Please remember to honor the local culture. Find out what works best for you and your project.

My journey, the next steps

After selling my house in September, I returned to Belize in November 2005 for ten days of setting up school visits in Belize City and Orange Walk Town. Orange Walk Town is one of six districts in Belize. Neftali, who planted the initial idea of literacy outreach, was from that area of the country and thus had connections to schools there. I first began with the school that my landlord's children attended—a personal connection is always helpful—and then expanded to the schools within walking distance of my room in Belize City. A few months later, I extended my daily range to Orange Walk Town because of Neftali's personal connections in that area.

The school visits consisted of literally showing up at the school and asking to speak to a principal or vice principal or a few teachers and then listening. I listened to their challenges, their needs, and their concerns. After listening, I shared what I had to offer as a person not connected to a university or Peace Corps or to any organization, just there on my own willing to offer enthusiasm, eight years experience as a children's librarian connecting books and children, and my passion for indigenous cultures. I entered every encounter with respect and seeking to understand. I made it clear that I did not have access to funding for large-scale programs. But I did have passion and a willingness to partner and share knowledge through some of the activities that worked in other schools and libraries for whom I had presented programs. I also had the desire to learn and adapt and apply that knowledge to a Belizean context.

Back in the US over the next two months, I began to study Belize, the country and its cultures through reading articles discovered in online research to learn more about their history, cultural norms, traditions, music, and celebrations. I researched the four most prominent cultures: Creole, Garifuna, Maya, and Mestizo.

Book Drives

My decision to do book drives started with requests from Belizean teachers in every school I visited for books for their classrooms. The need is great. In a typical grade one classroom, one might see a hand full of books, often cast-offs donated by tourists, covers torn, pages missing. Or you might see a few easy readers from a Barbie or Bob the Builder series. Teachers have very few local resources to purchase books for their classrooms. When I began traveling to Belize in 2005, there was not a single bookstore dedicated to selling *new* books. The books that were available were mostly overstock books from the US, often Hardy Boys and Nancy Drew. There is nothing wrong with either of those, but they are not helpful for children just beginning to read. There were many workbooks and coloring books available, but little in the way of quality reading materials.

The library system had no budget to purchase books and relied on the World Book Bank and the generosity of tourists and volunteers to fill their shelves. What I witnessed far too often was many people had good intentions but did not always think it through so they donated materials that Belizeans simply could not relate to. I was dismayed to see some of the books donated by well-meaning organizations such as the World Book Bank. At one location, I found three hundred boxes of books donated to the National Library Service. Within those boxes were encyclopedias from 1982 along with dozens and dozens of used algebra and American literature textbooks. If you lived in a small village, your reading skills were that of an eight or nine-year-old and your public library had only thirty books, would you want to read *those* books?

I began doing research on materials Belizeans *could* relate to: books about the rain forest, the coral reef (Belize is home to the second largest coral reef in the world), books about people of color whether African descent or Latino or Maya. I sought books in which Belizeans could see themselves in the stories or in the environment. And I started coordinating targeted book drives in the United States, requesting specific titles. Often, I found myself spending my own money to purchase books to donate to schools and libraries in Belize. The books were very well received. However, something was missing.

Incorporation of Training

As I continued traveling to various villages, I also learned Belizeans were eager and desperate for training on how to use the books donated. I always strove to ask, "What is it you *really* need?"

The response was, "Training, how to *use* the books. Many people give us books, but do not show us what we can do with them." I witnessed this first-hand; sometimes the books I donated were still in the same boxes untouched six months later. This was disheartening.

I asked why the books were not being used. "Miss, we cannot tell the stories like you do."

"But you *can* tell the stories like *you*," I responded emphatically. It became apparent there was a need for training. Somehow, I had to instill self-confidence and a belief in themselves that they could master the necessary skill set.

I developed several training manuals to pair with the sets of books I would donate. The manuals presented concrete ideas and lesson plans for how to use the books. They encouraged incorporating student participation, critical thinking questions and what I called "thinking outside the book"—how to add more than what was written on the page. There was an A-Z manual where each letter of the alphabet represented ideas to complement each one of the books donated. For example, *Diego Saves the Butterflies* discussed why butterflies are important in Belize and stressed the need to protect the environment. Further, it posed several critical thinking questions about why it is important to protect our environment and what students can do to help. One suggestion was that students write a few sentences about what the students could do to clean the environment at their own school or in their own neighborhood. The A-Z manual is included in the Appendices at the end of this book.

Next, I presented training sessions for teachers and librarians, which I called, *Bringing Books Alive Workshops*. I demonstrated how to use the donated materials and then left those materials behind, along with the training manuals. This made all the difference; when I returned for follow-up visits, the books were falling apart. That was a good thing because it meant they were being used! You can view those training videos on Youtube by searching Kristin Pedemonti Teacher Training or following this link: https://www.youtube.com/playlist?list=PLUSsJcb-fTHOeoX-NHVpm2MYvlUqTmpytR

I returned in January 2006 for my first extended trip. I established a base in Belize City and stayed for six weeks. Every day I visited schools, libraries, and universities. I listened, asked what I could do to help. Then, I shared what I felt competent to offer. One day, a chance visit to the main branch of the National Library Service in Belize City led to a deeper conversation and a partnership. It began with an afternoon of volunteering: helping to unpack, sort and catalog three hundred boxes of books donated by the World Book Bank. That led me to donate a few story hour programs for children at the library after school. As the library staff observed my story hours, the partnership evolved into a request to develop and deliver storytelling and *Bringing Books Alive Workshops* for librarians from twenty of the thirty-two library systems throughout the entire country. After I had shared those workshops, I was invited to participate as a storyteller and workshop facilitator in a national tour to fourteen village libraries from central coastal Belize down to far-flung Barranco, one of the southern-most villages. Barranco also happened to be the birthplace of Andy Palacio, the most famous and loved musician and keeper of Garifuna culture.

Another chance meeting—this one with a young professor—led to partnering and guest lecturing at the University of Belize for the Education Department and the teaching students.

During January and February, I presented storytelling and read-aloud programs at dozens of schools within Belize City. Then the floodgates opened. Through word of mouth, every week more and more teachers and principals were requesting me to come to their schools not only within Belize City but also in the surrounding villages. I had shared my Belize cell phone number and each week I would receive text message requests. Often, a teacher at a school where I was presenting would call her sister or cousin who taught at another school—and off I would go within a few days time to Burrell Boom or to Hattieville.

I traveled back and forth to Belize half a dozen times in 2005/2006, staying for up to six weeks at a time laying the groundwork for the project. As outlined above; I set up meetings with principals, teachers, librarians, university professors, officials in the Ministry of Education, other volunteers, villagers and potential sponsors. Every encounter was a chance to learn or meet someone who might know a teacher or a principal or an advocate for literacy who might want to partner with me or support the work in some way. The support came in various forms: promoting the project to other educators, informing a librarian about my work, sharing the project with a professor who might invite me to guest lecture or sharing my work with a local storyteller who might be interested in meeting me to share ideas.

There were many serendipitous moments like the time I was supposed to go to a school, but could not get a final confirmation so instead—on impulse—I went to a Rotary Club meeting. By chance, their speaker had just canceled. As I spoke to the president, he asked if I knew anyone who might be able to speak at the meeting which started in twenty minutes. I suggested that I could speak about my volunteer project. Amazingly enough, he agreed. I told the Rotarians about traveling to many schools, donating teacher training and literacy activities for the students. At that meeting, Rotarians donated exactly the amount I needed in order to stay another month! Chance encounters like that Rotary meeting happened so often that I came to think of Belize as having some sort of magic. In reality, the power most likely derived from my always putting myself out there and speaking enthusiastically about my project to anyone who would listen.

Make Every Day Count

I did my best to make every day count. I offered free storytelling for classrooms, modeling the use of books for the teachers and read-alouds for the children. I always left donated books behind. I offered teacher training sessions on *Bringing Books Alive in the Classroom* and *Storytelling in the Classroom* as I traveled school-to-school. Eventually, the National Belize Teacher's Union backed me with their endorsement of my work by supporting my project and allowing me to promote my workshops at their monthly meetings. Through that channel of promotion, I started offering sessions in different regions of the country for anywhere from twenty to eighty or more teachers. Those workshops led to invitations to present directly to other teachers and students at their schools. In the end, over eight hundred teachers participated in the training sessions. Now, they are training each other and offering the program in their own schools.

Doing the Right Thing—Yet Being Flexible

I tried diligently to do the "right thing." For example, going through proper channels and chain of command. Doing so often led to delays or to layers of bureaucracy and having meeting after meeting with numerous officials which sometimes circled back to more meetings without any results. Whenever following the chain of command did not work out as planned, I simply went directly to principals and teachers within schools and to staff at libraries. I asked a lot of questions about what the locals and teachers felt they actually needed.

The Big Move

After almost a year of traveling back and forth, it was time for the big move. In August 2006, I moved to Belize City, making it my base of operation from August 2006 to March 2007. I lived on Violet Lane in—unbeknownst to me—one of the worst neighborhoods in the city, riddled with violence from the Bloods and the Crips imported from Los Angeles. Los Angeles is often referred to as "Little Belize" because of the high numbers of Belizeans who have ended up immigrating there. The Los Angeles gangs realized an untapped drug market and thus flooded into Belize City. Sadly, the drug problem and gang violence escalated to the point that there were sometimes weekly shootings and retaliations. The saddest reality was the number of innocent people caught in the cross-fire. I suppose in some ways ignorance was bliss. Not realizing how severe the problem was, I did not live in fear or sequester myself in my room. I walked nearly everywhere I went. On those walks, I talked to as many Belizeans as possible—befriending taxi drivers, sanitation workers, the security guy at the corner grocery store, the women who owned and operated all the food shacks lining the main drag into downtown. I always felt safe. It felt like everyone had my back. James, the security guy at the grocery, told me that every evening he would watch to be sure I arrived at my room safely.

Lesson: Form relationships with locals. Become as much a part of the fabric of the community as possible. In so doing, not only will you learn a lot more about the local culture and life, but this will also form a layer of protection should anything go wrong.

I was lucky. My only negative experience in all my years in Belize was the run-in with ten young men, high out of their minds on crack, who surrounded me in Pink's Alley, which I learned later was the most dangerous street in Belize City.

When they asked, "White gyal, what you doing here?"

I responded, "I am going to that school right there," I pointed to Ethel Vargas Preschool about fifty yards in the distance, "and I am telling stories to the children."

The leader gestured to the others to move out of my way; it was like the Red Sea parting.

"Sorry Miss, all respect. Thank you for helping our children. Didn't know you was a teacher. You evah need protection, I got your back. Have a good day, Miss."

And they bowed their heads gesturing again for me to pass. I was astounded by their reaction—and grateful.

Day to Day Life

Every day I visited different schools, often showing up unannounced and explaining that I was a former librarian and now a storyteller with a passion for connecting children to books. Principals and teachers were usually open and eager to host literacy programs, sometimes on the very morning of my first appearance at a school. Frequently, on the very afternoon of my initial morning visit, I was invited to move from class to class, sharing stories. I presented storytelling programs and donated books to twenty-five schools and libraries in Belize City and surrounding villages.

Connections Further Outside the City

Within a few weeks, I began to make connections further outside the city via the National Library Service, which began recommending my work to other librarians in other districts. Teachers and principals recommended other schools for me to visit in other regions. Taxi drivers—and honestly anyone I met who learned I was developing a literacy project—would suggest I call their aunt who was a principal or their neighbor who was a teacher. I made those calls and received invitations to other regions of the country.

Where to Stay During Village Visits?

You may be wondering where I stayed during those visits. Every single visit, I was hosted by a teacher, a principal, or a family in the village where the school was located. I was treated with such kindness and compassion, I felt like royalty or a rock star. Sometimes the students would begin to argue over who would take me home that afternoon to feed and house me. It made my heart full to nearly bursting. I've slept in hammocks strung across one room with the entire family swinging each other to sleep. I've slept on sofas, on makeshift beds out of pillows, and even once or twice on a floor.

And the meals? Oh my goodness! I feasted on rice and beans and *escabeche* and homemade tortillas and eggs from chickens right in the yard. Sometimes my host would like to see if they could "get me," meaning could they get me to freak out over a particular dish. These were dishes such as *gibnut* (a rather large rodent which Belizeans sometimes barbecue). At those times I ate meat, and it was indeed delicious! I was also fed armadillo by a group of teachers in Burrell Boom who were convinced I would refuse. Nope, it was amazing, so tender! I was also given the head of the fish, this is considered a delicacy and an honor to receive. When a Belizean eats the head of the fish, the only bits left at the end are a few tiny pieces of bone and the lips. By the end of my time in Belize, you would have been hard-pressed to know who had stripped the flesh from a fish head, a Belizean or me. I felt like I truly belonged.

Partnerships Expanded

I was fortunate to volunteer with Rose Bradley and her CCETT program (Caribbean Center for Excellence in Teacher Training). The CCETT program was created to incorporate some of the Caribbean curricula into the Belizean schools and to reflect more of the local culture in reading programs. It was also designed to utilize books into subject areas in which the teachers were engaging their students. CCETT was supported by the Peace Corps as well. Workshops were presented to those who already taught in the Belizean school system as well as those in the education and teaching study programs at the University of Belize. I was invited to attend workshops and even offered to lead several workshops. The Peace Corps volunteers then helped connect me to other schools throughout Belize.

A bigger adventure began when I began traveling to dozens and dozens of villages to offer workshops and presentations in schools, libraries and universities. From the fall of 2006 into the winter of 2007, I presented programs throughout the country, spending much of my time in Orange Walk in the northern part of Belize and then out west in Cayo District. I traveled whenever and wherever anyone invited me. Some weeks I went to three or four villages. During this nearly a year, I believe I traveled to about fifty villages and over seventy-five schools.

Lesson: Be open to expanding your range. Be open to going where the invitations take you. Be open to saying, "YES," and figuring out logistics later.

Project Evolution: from the Printed Page to the Oral Tradition At this time, the thrust of the project began to change. The following section describes the next phases of the project's evolution.

Connecting Culture

The next step of Literacy Outreach Belize evolved as I was traveling village to village. Belizeans began to share their own indigenous legends with me. I was grateful for the trust they placed in me, a non-Belizean. Their openness and willingness to share their stories with me brought smiles to my face. It made me feel more accepted that Belizeans would tell me their tales. I felt validated in the work I was doing, the connections I was making person to person as I traveled and listened and learned. In one school, teachers and students told me tales of *Tata Duende*, a dwarf with twisted backward feet who serves as protector of the rain forest. In another village, I heard tales of *Xtabai*, a shape-shifter. A beautiful woman by day who searches for drunken men to lure into the forest where she transforms into a horrible serpent-like monster and attacks. *El Cadejo,* a shape-shifting devil-hound represents the battle between good and evil. In many villages, I was treated to vivid retellings of *La Llorona,* the crying woman who wanders by the riverside searching for her lost children. More about this in Chapter Two.

As I heard these tales throughout Belize I realized they could be powerful tools to:

> ‣ Connect the four most prominent cultures: the Creole, Garifuna, Maya and Mestizo within the classrooms.

> ‣ Build bridges between the cultures and students through their own stories.

> ‣ Create a lesson plan in which the students and teachers could see themselves reflected—rather than outside influences.

I began asking teachers, librarians, storyteller Myrna Manzanares, and people I met on my travels through the country if they knew any of these legends and if would they be comfortable sharing their stories with me. To my delight, they were. In the homes of Belizeans in small villages such as San Lazaro, San Felipe, Burrell Boom, Bullet Tree Falls, even in Belize City, and out on the Isle of Caye Caulker, people shared their stories.

Ninety-nine percent of the time there was no formal procedure for collecting the stories. I did not want to hinder the flow of conversation or introduce a potential barrier to sharing by thrusting a recorder into a villager's face or taking notes. And so I listened and then afterward I recorded as best I could on paper with a pen what I had heard. There were times I asked for permission to use a recorder or take notes. Often I would listen in the moment and then later ask for a certain part to be repeated, or I would ask clarifying questions while taking notes.

In Belize, these tales are told with profound respect by most for these are not simply stories; these are encounters with real spirits who serve to teach important lessons. The stories I collected present lessons such as protecting and preserving the rain forest, fidelity, obeying one's parents, respect for each other, the dangers of drinking to excess, and thinking before we act. All of these are lessons that are perfect teaching tools for the classroom. And yet, the stories were missing from most of the schools. It was not until January of 2012, while filming what was to be a documentary but transformed into two teacher-training videos, that I learned about the ban.

Banned in Belize *or* Sometimes Ignorance is Bliss

Sometimes one's own ignorance is a form of bliss. I had no idea that for five years I was being a rebel with a cause by sharing *banned legends* in the schools. No one told me about the ban until January of 2012, when it was mentioned at one of the teacher training workshops in San Ignacio, Cayo District. The very stories I had begun collecting, the same stories that helped students find meaning in their lessons, presented a complex issue. I was told that some schools banned the stories because of religious reasons and because many misunderstood the meaning of the stories.

This misunderstanding is complicated. Many of the

legendary figures are spirits like *La Llorona* and *Tata Duende*, which were considered by some of the churches and their leaders who supported and constructed some of the schools to be in some way Satanic or evil. However, the messages and lessons of the stories echoed many socially-desirable lessons. They taught morals that are even commandments in many religions: fidelity, honoring one's mother and father, keeping oneself free from gluttony. But because the figures were in spirit form, the legends were banned.

I was also told that the legends were banned from being told when the British were in power. Sadly, this happens nearly every time one country is colonized by another. Those in political and economic control understand that our stories carry great power—as does our language. One form of suppression of a people or culture is to take away their language and their stories. When the British were in political power, English was the official language of business, education, and politics. This continues until today.

As for the stories, many Belizeans I spoke to told me that they were told that their indigenous stories and legends were silly and simplistic. Their cultural stories were made fun of and dishonored. When our stories are dishonored it affects us more deeply than we may realize; it chips away at pride, self-esteem, and self-worth.

There were many reasons no one told me about the ban. Although I was accepted and well received at workshops, as a white American woman I was still an outsider, and it would have been considered rude to tell me I was doing something wrong.

Add to this the sad reality of the colonial mentality—that of a people whose own languages and stories were suppressed or even banned—and there continued to be a pervasive belief that outside ideas were somehow superior or that an educator or storyteller from the outside was superior to native ideas or teachers. Thus, I was allowed to continue the work I was doing. There was also a sort of saving face. Belizeans did not want to appear as being inconsiderate to an outsider. I have observed a common concern throughout the entire world—one culture or people not wanting to appear inferior or negative to another. And it is understandable. So, for five years I presented workshops using indigenous legends—having no clue I was breaking rules.

Connecting a Challenge to Cultural Stories

Though Belize prides itself on being harmonious, I witnessed a definite hierarchy between the cultures, as well as mistrust and even bullying. The indigenous stories seemed to be a perfect vehicle to break down barriers between the cultures and perhaps dismantle the hierarchy. If the stories were shared with teachers and students, perhaps they could see that across cultures they had similar stories. That insight would show them that they were not so different from each other as they thought—and that their native stories held valuable lessons. If those stories were valued, then perhaps their cultures would be more deeply appreciated. Then—in turn—perhaps the students and teachers would value themselves as well. It was a leap, but one that I felt was worth taking.

And so I continued to learn as much as I could about the

legends from books, locals, anyone who was willing to share information. Over several months I developed a simple creative writing exercise using the indigenous legends. That exercise is described in step-by-step detail in Chapter Three.

Lesson: What you set out to do may change drastically over time. Be willing to adapt.

The creative writing exercise was more impactful than I ever could have hoped, even from the very first session. And for many reasons. The students and teachers could see themselves in the material. They could see that an outsider (whom for whatever reason, they respected) was valuing their indigenous culture. They could see the cross-cultural connections. Students and teachers were engaged in the workshops and deeply connected to the lesson. They wrote short stories that may have been lacking in correct grammar and spelling but were wildly creative. They participated with enthusiasm. Grammar and spelling can be taught, often creativity cannot. Because of the enthusiastic student and teacher response, I realized this lesson contained something special.

From 2008 through 2012 the focus became perfecting and presenting the workshop *Using Indigenous Stories in the Classroom to Teach Creative Writing* to teachers, teachers in training and students. That presentation and workshop also changed over time. The entire evolution of the project is explained in greater detail in the next section.

⤸

The Power of Stories

Stories hold great power: to connect us one to another, to unite us and build strength, to share history, to share cultural mores, to share a group's traditions, language, and life-lessons. People in government know this. All throughout the world, cultural stories have been systematically taken away from indigenous peoples as a way to squelch their power, destroy their sense of place, sense of self, and sense of belonging. If you take someone's culture, you strip them of more than the story; you steal their pride. This runs deeper than many may imagine. I witnessed this first hand in Belize—a country where people in the villages knew and shared their stories, at least with each other, and at least until a few decades ago.

In many villages, locals told me that outsiders poked fun at their stories and told them the indigenous legends they shared were not real. Little value was placed on preserving these stories, with the exception of a handful of academics. Many schools were banned from using their own cultural stories within the classrooms. They may have shared *Anansi* stories, but *Anansi* is not Belizean. *Anansi* stories were brought over from Western Africa and the Caribbean. Some teachers shared the occasional *Tata Duende* tale focusing on his message of protecting and preserving the rain forest. But most of the other legends were missing. And I felt something must be done to change that.

The Importance of Asking Questions and Listening

What I thought I was going to do was *not* what ultimately

happened. The project evolved over time and involved asking countless questions and deeply listening to what the Belizean people truly needed and wanted from me. I kept asking, "How could I best serve your village, school, or library?" This sincere inquiry was absolutely imperative to the success and full reception of the project. The formula I learned was:

1. Involve the locals
2. Ask questions
3. Listen
4. And then do

Literacy Outreach Belize changed significantly over the years because of what Belizeans requested of me. I believe it has been so well received because *I listened* and did my best to offer what was asked. Whether the need was for book drives, librarian training, methods for using donated materials, or assistance with creative writing, I made it happen as often as possible.

The inclusion of their indigenous cultural legends arose after countless conversations in dozens of villages and the realization of how powerful the legends could be as teaching tools in the classrooms.

Here's what I witnessed too often: outsiders come in thinking they have all the answers on how to solve the problems. They do not.

Problems are usually multifaceted, tied into culture, economics, social stratification, colonialism, et cetera, and problems run deeper than what may initially appear. This is why building relationships and gaining trust is crucial. I found that the most effective introduction was asking the difficult questions and active listening as I heard the honest responses. It is important to respect and honor the culture(s) with which you are working. Every culture has value and something to teach us. Listen. Respect. And be willing to evolve. This is key.

Challenges as Opportunities for Growth and Change

Before I share the nuts and bolts of the lesson plan that came out of my experience in Belize, let me recount some of the challenges Literacy Outreach Belize faced. These challenges are similar in many developing countries. Perhaps my experience in overcoming some of these obstacles may help you in replicating this program or in creating your own.

Challenge: Colonial Mentality

As I traveled throughout Belize, another realization occurred. Because Belize is a young country, the colonial mentality continues to be pervasive. This is through no fault of the Belizeans, but because of what was systematically done to them. For decades they were controlled by an outside power, the British, who often led Belizeans to believe that their own cultures were somehow second-rate, not good enough, and that outside influence and ideas were superior to their own. This is a problem in nearly every country that has been colonized. In Belize, it created a people who were dependent on outsiders to provide answers, people who mistrusted their own ideas. Sadly, this cycle is perpetuated for a multitude of reasons. Two of the primary reasons are the history of the country and the many volunteers and outside organizations who establish projects to help but do not always involve Belizeans in the development of the project. That kind of insensitivity and cultural disconnection continues the cycle of thinking that outsiders must be needed to solve local problems.

Solution: Be Mindful and Focus on Confidence-Building and Stereotype-Breaking

I was always mindful of this internal conflict. Was I perpetuating the cycle, too? I believe it is why I constantly asked for Belizeans to be involved in what I was doing. I made a point of asking what they felt they needed rather than making any assumption that I knew what they needed. It is also why at every training I started with, "I have a deep love of Belize and its cultures. I do not have all the answers. I have a lot of enthusiasm, and I have a few ideas. *You have many of the answers within you,* all you need is someone to help pull them out of you and build your own confidence."

I did my best to build bridges and utilize Belizean culture in the lessons and training I shared. Even in what may seem a very small way, for example, taking a song like "If You're Happy and You Know it, Clap your Hands" and doing something so seemingly simple as adding Belizean cultural references. "If you're happy and you know it, dance the Punta." The Punta is a Belizean dance. This often led to laughter, especially as I danced. But it also illustrated that I knew about Belizean culture and that I respected it.

On a side note, I made friends with Belizeans wherever I lived or traveled. I noticed that many times volunteers came in, but did not seem to spend much time with the Belizean people outside of the projects upon which they were working. I was incredibly fortunate to have friends with whom to spend time on the weekends, to go dancing, to experience so many facets of Belizean culture. How much can you truly learn about a culture if you do not fully immerse yourself? How can you build relationships if you do not open your heart?

Challenge: Educational System

There are many challenges in Belize related to their educational system. It is a somewhat antiquated system, notably utilizing memorization by rote, response in unison. This system was put into place when the British were in power and continues to this day. In my observation of primary schools throughout every district in Belize, the teacher writes *everything* on the chalkboard, the students learn by parroting back their responses in unison. There are too few textbooks. Thus the students have notebooks for every subject, in which the teacher writes each lesson by hand, often taking half the class time to write the problems or questions the students are to solve. Much of the work is fill-in-the-blank or multiple-choice, and there is little room for free writing or expression. Through no fault of the teachers, learning disabilities or differences often go undiagnosed, and students are passed to the next grade level whether or not they can truly do the work; a frustration for both student and teacher.

Curriculum

The primary school curriculum does not entirely prepare

the students for the rigors of the high school curriculum. Primary school is memorization by rote, multiple choice, and fill in the blank. At some schools, a few stories or themes are assigned in the two years leading up to high school. The high school curriculum is primarily essay writing. This system sets the students up for failure. According to UNESCO, sixty-three percent of Belizean children enroll in Secondary School. This is nearly equal to the percentage of students who pass the National Exam. This is indeed a sad reality. Nearly forty percent of students do not go beyond a seventh-grade education. In Belize, education is compulsory only to the completion of primary school or what is equal to grade seven.

Challenge: The Need for Teacher Training

Until 2009, Belizeans could graduate from high school, take two weeks of training in the summer and become a teacher. As of 2009, a new law requires new teachers to have completed a two-year degree in education. This is a welcome and significant change to the system.

Solution: Tap into Training Programs

Learn how you can partner with existing programs and promote your work too. Often the newer teacher training programs at universities are looking for innovative teaching ideas or projects. I was invited to three different universities to guest lecture and share workshops with their education departments.

Challenge: Teaching in Tough Circumstances: ESL, Special Needs Students, Large Class Size, Relocation/Consistency

A Belizean teacher's task is enormous. Nearly no one in Belize speaks English at home. Approximately seventy percent of the population speaks Belizean Creole, a substrate of English, or they speak Garifuna, Spanish, or one of three Maya dialects. Classrooms often contain thirty-five to forty students, and each student possesses a different level of English language skills, as well as learning differences which the teacher must tackle solo without any teacher aides. To top it off, most of the schools are concrete block buildings in which sound bounces and reverberates. The absence of carpeting or other sound-absorbing materials means that classrooms are cacophonous environments filled with student and teacher voices from not only one classroom, but also those surrounding. I am impressed with how teachers are able to focus and teach effectively in this environment.

Finally, teachers are often relocated from school to school or region to region. The reasons for these moves are many, and include:

> Politics
> Punishment of a teacher
> The thought that a good teacher can spread his or her teaching methods to another school.

As a result of so much disruption, there is seldom time to build up consistency and coherency within any one school or in working with one particular population. Belizean teachers work in relatively tough circumstances.

Solution: Be aware of the challenges faced by the teachers with whom you are working.

Take these challenges into consideration. Should you become frustrated by what you might think of as a lack of interest on behalf of teachers, remember that they are often simply overwhelmed with the task at hand.

Challenge: Economics

Although Belizean primary school is free, the textbooks, compulsory school uniforms, school fees and in some cases even a student's desk or chair cost money. The textbooks can be quite expensive, even cost-prohibitive for some families. In some villages, students are only expected to finish primary school and then begin working for the family. However, in much of my travels and my experience in Belize, it became apparent that economic issues were not usually the primary reason a child dropped out before high school. What I witnessed most frequently was the students not being able to pass the national exam to enter high school because of the issues in the educational system previously described.

Solution: Be aware of the economic realities of school in the developing world. It is not free.

Sensitivity to expenses borne by struggling families, underfunded schools, and overstretched educational systems is needed when encountering teaching environments around the world.

Turning Challenges into Opportunities—
Incorporating All I'd Learned Into a Lesson Plan

The project took all of these realities into consideration:

> ➤ Being mindful of trying to not add to a teacher's burden.
> ➤ Understanding the variations in teachers' training.
> ➤ Observing class size challenges.
> ➤ The task of teaching to a very wide range of student ability.
> ➤ ESL and special needs issues.
> ➤ Financial challenges faced by students and teachers.

Being aware of the myriad dynamics meant being more open to discussion and adaptation. It also meant making no assumptions about their level of involvement in the project. It also meant that as the program evolved over time, I focused much farther down and into a select and a small number of schools in which the teachers and principals were highly invested in the project and became champions and full partners.

After learning indigenous legends from every region of Belize and realizing the connections between the various cultures and the need for Belizeans to see *themselves* in the material utilized in school, those legends seemed perfect teaching tools for the classroom. Besides, the excitement generated by use of local legends became a uniting factor between the students and teachers. Thus, in January of 2007, upon the request from teachers that I develop a writing program to assist them with lesson plans to prepare their students for the Primary School Exam—that students are required to take in order to enter high school—I developed a simple creative writing exercise using these legends.

Many of the legends cross cultures and beautifully illustrate our interconnectedness. I thought it would be a perfect lesson in bridging the cultures together. Belize likes to promote itself as a harmonious place, and in many ways it is. However, because of my many Belizean friends—from every cultural group—I witnessed frequent episodes of mistrust between the cultures. It became evident that a definite hierarchy existed with the Creole and Garifuna at the top followed by Mestizo and Maya on the bottom. In this social environment, I wanted to illustrate the humanity we all share. The country's indigenous legends seemed an obvious resource to show the population's common ground.

Why Indigenous Stories are Important in Connecting Culture, Classroom and Community

Basic Outline of the Indigenous Story Program

And so the program evolved from the initial book drives and training focused around print materials to the development of a simply structured three-paragraph creative writing exercise based on the indigenous legends that were familiar across the Belizean cultural groups. The basic idea was that students would introduce one of the legendary figures, describe that character and the setting of their story in paragraph one, and then in paragraphs two and three describe what would happen, moment-by-moment, if they met that legend face-to-face.

The lesson would begin with a discussion of the four most

popular and prominent legends: *Tata Duende, Xtabai, La Llorona* and *El Cadejo*. Each one portrays positive lessons and morals that are perfect for the classroom: environmental awareness, respect, obeying parents, not drinking to excess, fidelity, parents being mindful of their children. We focused on these legends because of the depth of their messages and the fact that many of them are not as widely known, due to the reasons described earlier: the ban of the legends in many schools as well as the disrespect of the legends by outsiders and even some of those in power within Belize. Although after years of research, I discovered how widespread *La Llorona* and *Duende* legends are throughout Central and South America, once again illustrating our interconnectedness.

At first, I had also included *Anansi* as he was perhaps the most widely known legend across all of the cultures. Later, I decided to focus on the other lesser-known—though equally important and impactful—legends which deserved to be preserved. In my opinion, the *Anansi* stories were being shared and preserved so there was little danger they would be lost, whereas the other cultural legends were not being shared in many of the schools.

Though as a side note, I did often tell an *Anansi* story I learned in Creole, *Wai Nani Goat Tayl Kungku (Why Nanny Goat's Tail is Short)* by Gladys Stewart. We discussed how *Anansi* always used his brains to trick others, often characters bigger than himself. Brains are more important than brawn. This is positive. We reviewed the symbolism of the *Anansi* stories. Even if one is socially or economically disadvantaged, one can, with the use of clever wit, pull up and out of current circumstances. **Note:** Chapter Three goes into step by step, scripted detail of how to present and adapt to your needs.

Student Engagement

The students responded with enthusiasm and excitement; they were engaged in this material because they could see themselves represented in the lessons presented. These legends are regarded quite seriously in many of the villages. There is a respect and honor paid to the tales. In fact, for many these are not simply stories, they are real life figures that serve to warn us about the ramifications and consequences of our negative behavior.

Often, in-depth discussions were held about the various details in the stories. Sometimes arguments even arose: "*Xtabai* has clear skin, green eyes, she live in da bush, she have long, long light color hair."

Another student disagrees, "No di tru, she got long, long black hair, dark eyes, you see she by da roadside."

And then I interject, "you are both correct, *Xtabai* looks different depending on where in Belize you see her." The students were astounded. More so when I shared that *Xtabai* stories are found in both Maya and Mestizo culture.

The same goes for *Tata Duende*, protector of the rain forest. His description varies depending on which region in Belize you hear the story. In some parts of the country he is described as always wearing the color red, other places he is dressed in brown. But two details are always the same, his twisted "backway" feet and his thumbless hands. The Maya also have a version of *Tata*

Duende called *Alux*. He is only one foot tall. When he plays his magic trumpet-like horn, it casts a spell on the listener—sending him into a deep slumber. Both *Tata Duende* and *Alux* protect the rain forest or "bush." Further details about each legend will be presented in Chapter Two.

These legends are viewed as real spirits—not myths—in Belizean culture, as well as in many cultures throughout the world. These stories are based on real experiences and actual people and events from days gone by. The culture has expanded upon and exaggerated those events over time, resulting in the legends we know today. Perhaps the legend of *Tata Duende* truly is based upon a man who was born with a deformity, twisted backward feet, who only grew to three feet in height. Perhaps his difference in appearance was unaccepted in his village, and he endured years of taunts. Eventually, he ventured out of the village to live in the forest because he felt so ostracized by society. Perhaps after time in the forest he realized that animals do not judge by appearance, they judge by the content of character. So *Tata Duende* befriended the animals and for the first time in his life, he felt accepted. Thus he became the protector of the forest who teaches others to respect the environment. If one views *Tata Duende,* the guardian of the rain forest as a real person this provides the potential for the listener to connect to the character more empathetically. Every one of these legends has valuable lessons and wisdom.

After my time spent living in Belize, I moved back to the USA. Even so, I continued to return to Belize for at least one month each year from 2007 up until 2012. During those visits

I shared follow-up workshops with five or six schools, closely working with staff and students as well as presenting teacher-training workshops throughout the country in different regions.

By the time the program ended in February of 2012, I had been to over seventy-five villages all over the country. I had been housed by dozens of teachers and families. Over thirty-three thousand students received free literacy programs—whether read-alouds, interactive folktale presentations or creative writing workshops.

Hundreds of teachers attended and participated in the *Bringing Books Alive* and *How to Use Indigenous Stories to Teach Creative Writing* workshops. The best part is the program continues as teachers use the lessons shared and have trained each other. Terry Ulloa, one of the first librarians I met, trains other librarians and teachers, not only in Belize, but also throughout the Caribbean. I am so honored to know the seeds planted have sprouted and spread!

Six Tips and Some Thoughts

First and foremost: listen to the people you are serving. The number one request I hear from the people with whom I work and collaborate all across the globe—whether Belize, Ghana, Haiti, Kenya, Poland, or inner city or rural schools of the USA—is, "Please tell people to listen to us; we have ideas, we have intelligence. Being poor does not mean we are stupid or without potential solutions to our own challenges. Being poor may mean lacking certain resources, it may mean needing collaboration to bring our ideas to fruition, but please listen because we are rich in ideas."

And so I learned to ask respectfully, realizing that, by listening fully, I would earn the trust of communities and be able to help them more intelligently. I came to understand that every encounter is an opportunity to learn. While observing other outsiders inability to fully partner with their less respectful attitudes, I learned to listen to the people I was serving.

Should you choose to reach out to a less-developed culture, you will be well advised to listen to the people you are teaching. Listen to the children. Listen to the elders. Listen to the teachers, parents, and community. Listen to educational authorities, though they may be invested in the status quo. We each have much to learn from each other. Not a single one of us has all the answers. It is through listening that we learn and grow. It is through listening that a good project or idea can become a great project or idea. It is through listening that we can learn what is truly needed in a classroom, community or culture. Listening is one of the main reasons this literacy project was so well received, respected and requested throughout Belize. Listening well was the skill that caused me to be invited to Ghana and inner city and rural communities in the US.

Second and as important: be willing to adapt your ideas or project to the needs of the people you are serving. You may have what seems to be the best idea or project. You may have worked and researched for months before offering it to a particular group or population. While your idea probably has great value, no amount of individual study, thought, or analysis can replace respectful, focused listening to those you propose to serve. Not discounting your earnest preparation, it is extremely important to be willing to adapt your idea or change your project according to the needs of the people. Prepare through research, absolutely. Then be prepared to further educate yourself by hearing from client populations. Listening is first, and then the willingness to adapt and apply is second. Both are imperative to your project and to your being received and respected. It is also simply the right thing to do.

Third: Value the culture of those you are serving. It is important to value and respect the culture and people you are serving. For success in a cross-cultural project, the donor must approach the client and culture with deep respect. Keep in mind that the client populace is most likely advancing every year, and has been doing so for generations without your advice. Their ideas deserve as much value and respect as your own.

Remember that the people you are serving have a wealth of life experience to share. Learn about the culture either before you arrive or take the time when you first come to learn as much as you can by listening and by asking questions. Learn by creating relationships with the people you are serving. If they invite you to their nephew's fifth birthday party ceremony, go and learn about how they celebrate compared to how you do. If they invite you to church, go with an open mind and heart. If they want to share a traditional food with you, try it. If they want to teach you how to make a traditional recipe, watch and learn. Knowing, valuing, and respecting the culture of the people you are serving will bode well for you as you encounter potential challenges.

Sometimes these challenges are simply cultural differences—no right or wrong, just different. Being aware of local customs from the outset will make your life easier, your time on site more effective, and will probably ease the journey.

Fourth: Persevere one day, one conversation, one school, one village at a time. This is a *one day at a time* process. It is about putting yourself out there, one day, one conversation, one school, and one village at a time. Realizing it was a one day at a time process made all the difference for me. If one school said no, I knew there were dozens of others in Belize City alone that might say yes. Though I did get discouraged at times, fortunately, there were only a handful of nos. In fact, there were so many yesses it was a challenge to accommodate them all without burning out. In hindsight, I should have built in breaks to rest and recoup. I recommend taking some time to explore and not work. My own regimen was usually to work six days a week resting completely on Sundays. This pace worked for me, but is not for everyone.

Fifth: Conversations, not monologues. When you schedule a meeting, remember that your project is not all about you. Your project must be focused on the teachers and students it is designed to serve. Even your planning session is not about you, it is about having a conversation. It is appropriate to open the planning meeting with a succinct statement about what you believe you have to offer.

Then *you listen* to what their needs are to see if the two fit together. During my time in Belize, I participated in hundreds of conversations in which I asked questions such as how could I best serve, given my skill set. Sharing my experience—a love of story, eight years experience as a children's librarian, my theater background, my basic understanding and passion for storytelling, and my appreciation for indigenous stories—always seemed to win the day.

Sixth: The big picture, you've got the idea, now take action and show up. Begin with your idea and take action. For me, it started with one school visit to Muffles College in Orange Walk Town. That one visit resulted in other visits to the schools within walking distance of my residence in Belize City. I had no particular plan. Each day I would simply show up at a school after the school had been in session for about an hour and a half. I would ask to speak to the principal or some of the primary teachers and have conversations about my skill set. After I had shared what I could offer and gauged their interest, we would discuss more about what they needed. Every face-to-face discussion was a learning experience for me. I chose to show up in person rather than call or send an email or a letter because I learned that, in this particular culture, face-to-face meant a better chance of something happening. I was showing more commitment. They could see my face, I could see theirs. I became a real human being rather than words on a page. They could hear my enthusiasm and my heart. I could understand their challenges or their needs more clearly. Body language—especially facial gestures—and tone of voice communicated volumes during these initial visits. The approach I developed was the opposite of anonymous. It was completely human. I fully believe that this is part of the reason Literacy Outreach Belize was so successful.

CHAPTER TWO

Legends of Belize—Shapeshifters & Spirits

Tata Duende

Perhaps the most prevalent of Belizean legends is *Tata Duende*, the protector of the forest. *Tata* means old man or grandfather in Maya and *duende* is dwarf in Spanish. The *Tata Duende* stories are found in every region of Belize as well as throughout Central and South America, with variations in the title character's physical description depending on where the story is told. *Tata Duende* is the traditional guardian angel of all animals and people of the forest. A kind creature by nature, he is often said to feed, protect, and cure people hurt or lost in the forest. He is a close friend to the animals and punishes hunters that kill more game than they need.

In Belize, *Tata Duende* is described as being about three feet tall with twisted backward feet and no thumbs. He wears tattered clothing—often red in color or animal skins—a huge sombrero that nearly covers his eyes, and carries a machete. He is an excellent guitar player, and many children say he also loves the game of marbles. I found these two facts interesting, particularly since he is described as having no thumbs. He lives in the "bush" or forest where he protects the animals from over-hunting and the plants from deforestation. It is said that if you hear whistling far away, *Tata Duende* is nearby. If you hear whistling nearby, no worries, he is far away. Many of the stories warn people to not take more than they need from the forest: to conserve, preserve, and respect nature.

Older generations spoke of meeting up with *Tata Duende* in the rain forest, especially the men who worked as chichleros, those who harvested *chichle*—which was then processed into chewing gum—from the trees. They spoke of seeing a small man with twisted feet in the rain forest, where they claimed that he sometimes took their possessions or teased them with whistling and then disappeared.

I heard many stories about *Tata Duende* throughout my travels. Many stories were recounted to me as direct experiences of *Duende* as a trickster. I heard countless tales of *Tata Duende* hiding personal possessions, breaking dishware, routing through a garden, and the ubiquitous plaiting of the horse's hair. *Tata Duende* is a trickster who appears in and around people's homes, making mischief of one kind or another. I heard many tales in Bullet Tree Falls from Naida, a Creole and Mestizo woman who was one of the cherished staff members at the Parrot Nest, an inn that was my home base in western Belize. She would share with me how *Duende* visited her home in the early morning, plaiting the hair of her horse's mane and tail in such tight knots she would never be able to untangle them. I heard similar stories in Caye Caulker, San Lazaro, and Burrel Boom, villages where the residents would not have had much opportunity to interact with people from other villages as they are rather far apart and not readily accessible.

Tata Duende is also the protector of the rain forest and there are countless stories of him appearing when need be to honor the forest and its inhabitants—whether plant or animal. I heard stories of hunters who were taking more than their fair share and *Tata Duende* appeared to scold them, remind them to respect the animals, and take only what they needed. Often he would cast spells on them in which they would have no memory of their actions, but would awake with a new-found respect for the environment.

Children shared their encounters, too. They told of hearing whistling in the bush, going out to investigate and seeing nothing, but being so intrigued by the sound that they followed it until they got lost. Other children shared stories of their parents telling them that, if they cried, *Duende* would come and get them and "lose them in the bush." A few children spoke about items in their homes being misplaced by *Duende*. Always, they shared stories of horses manes and tails being plaited with knots, the "handiwork" of *Duende*.

Lessons: *Tata Duende* teaches respect for the environment including the forest and animals, to not over hunt or take more than we need. The stories preach conservation and preservation of natural resources. On a deeper level, they also teach us to accept those different than ourselves or experience the repercussions: to be compassionate and not judge a book by its cover.

Xtabai, Maya

Some say that *Xtabai* is similar to the Sirens of Greek lore, but rather than lure sailors to the sea, Xtabai leads men into the depths of the forest.

Xtabai, a legend from the Maya, is a shape-shifter: a beautiful woman by day with long flowing hair, a gorgeous body, and alluring personality. Although she has a deformity and is often described as having a goat or chicken foot or leg. She has the ability to morph into any woman's appearance she pleases. Her description varies depending upon which region the legends are told. I first heard of her as a woman with "clear" (white) skin, green eyes and long light colored hair. In most other versions, she was described as having long black hair, brown skin (Maya) and dark eyes. In either case, every story describes her great beauty, at least during the day. She spends her time beneath the Ceiba tree, which is sacred in Maya culture, patiently waiting for men to lure into the forest where she transforms into a horrible, serpent-like monster and attacks or devours the men. If the men survive the initial attack, they often become ill with a high fever. Some say that one can protect oneself from *Xtabai* by making the sign of the cross or praying. This protection applies to most of the legends in Belize except *El Cadejo*.

Most often *Xtabai* preys upon drunken men who are contemplating cheating on their wives or girlfriends. Her transformation varies. In some stories, they say she has a hole in her back and her skin is rough like the bark of a tree; this is where she hides her spines during the day. Others say her head transforms to that of a horse's head, scales rip out down her back, and her nails lengthen into long claws as sharp as razors. Some stories say she can also transform into a snake or a prickly tree and when in the form of a tree she pierces the long prickles through the man mortally wounding him.

In any case, she is a warning to men to behave, to be faithful to their wives or girlfriends or deal with her wrath. Men spoke of being put under a spell by her beauty, unable to control their own actions and unwillingly following wherever she would lead them. There is a saying, "Hell hath no fury like a woman scorned." *Xtabai* certainly seems to fit the bill.

There are many legends about why *Xtabai* turned into a monster. The stories I heard told of how her husband cheated on her and in her anger she attacked or killed him. And now she seeks out other men who are contemplating cheating on their wives or girlfriends to teach them a lesson. Most of the stories I heard were not about why *Xtabai* did what she did, no back-story, but only described her current attacks or seeing her by the Ceiba tree in their own villages.

I've heard several stories of *Xtabai*, from children who say they saw her by the Ceiba tree, waiting for someone to attack. A female student at Immaculate Conception school in Bullet Tree Falls recounted how *Xtabai* stood by the Ceiba tree in her yard night after night waiting for her older brother. Finally, out of concern for their son's safety, the family chopped down the Ceiba tree. *Xtabai* disappeared and never returned.

In the book *Characters and Caricatures of Belize,* compiled by Meg Craig in 1991, it is written that there was a beautiful Maya woman of the aristocratic family with whom all of the men in the village fell in love including a handsome noble. Another woman in her village, an enchantress was also in love with the noble man and placed a spell on the beautiful woman that she would entice and throw herself at all the men in the village including the nobleman in order to turn the nobleman against her. Her behavior angered everyone, and she eventually lived on her own in the forest where she died.

My Own Encounter

I had my very own encounter with *Xtabai,* on a bus. While traveling to a relatively remote village in Toledo District Southern Belize, I was on a local bus, the only white person in a sea of beautiful Maya and Mestizo faces. I noticed two little girls pointing at me, with wide eyes, they were whispering, *"Xtabai! Xtabai!"* I had only been in Belize a short while at the time and had no idea what they were referring to. I asked several people on the bus if they knew who or what *Xtabai* was. Nearly no one spoke English, or if they did, they did not answer me. A woman sitting two rows behind me began to laugh. Finally she spoke, *"Xtabai* is legend here. She look a lot like you, long blonde hair, clear skin, green eyes. A beautiful woman by day." I interjected, "Oh, thank you." I spoke too soon as she replied, "Oh, gyal wait 'til you hear what happens. At night she transform into one ugly serpent monstah, scales down her back and long, long claws. She got one leg of da chicken or goat. She attack men and sometime thief (steals) children."

Well, now I understood why those two little girls were so frightened. I did the only thing I could think to do, I got up, made my way into the aisle of the bus, pulled up my pants legs and showed them my legs. I pointed to my legs and said, "no chicken, no, bwaack bwaack." They stopped crying. I pointed to myself and smiled, "I'm Kristin, no *Xtabai*." They smiled, too. And the rest of the bus ride was peaceful though punctuated by a bit of laughter. All was well until I arrived at the school. As soon as I walked into the Kindergarten classroom, the children pointed and wide-eyed I could hear the whispers, "*Xtabai! Xtabai!*" Here we go again!

Lessons: *Xtabai* teaches lessons of fidelity, remaining faithful to one's wife or girlfriend and respecting women in general. She also teaches about not drinking to excess or the potential perils of doing so.

La Llorona, Mestizo

La Llorona is a legend widely known throughout Mexico, Central, and South America. She is so famous in this region that there are entire books and movies about her. In Belize, *La Llorona* is described as a beautiful woman with long tangled black hair that covers her tear-stained face. She always wears a long white gown. It is said that sometimes she appears to float. She is usually seen by the riverside where she searches for her lost children. *La Llorona* forever mourns the children she drowned in the river.

The reasons why she drowned her children vary from

region to region and country to country. Some of the legends in Belize say that *La Llorona's* husband often traveled and was away for extended periods of time. *La Llorona* became lonely and had an affair from which she became pregnant. She gave birth and of course the baby looked nothing like her husband. To avoid his anger, she drowned the child. Rather than be appeased, her husband was horrified by her actions and left her. In her despair, she drowned herself. Other legends say that it was her husband who had the affair and in her anger at his actions, to spite him, she drowned his children. Once again her actions had the opposite effect of what she had hoped; he left her and in her grief over the loss of her children and her spouse, she drowned herself. In all of the legends shared, *La Llorona* weeps by the riverside searching for the children she drowned.

Perhaps the most poignant version I heard was from a twelve-year-old boy in Bullet Tree Falls who told me he heard that *La Llorona* did not drown her children out of malice but out of mercy; that the family was quite poor and did not have enough food to eat. To spare the children the prolonged anguish of starving to death, she drowned them. Forever after she wanders the riverside searching for their lost souls or for other children to replace the ones she drowned.

Other children shared more innocent versions of the story as well. *La Llorona* was simply not minding her children and by complete accident, they fell into the river and drowned. And thus she is forever searching for them.

The *La Llorona* stories I heard were often very brief encounters of seeing a woman in a white dress floating nearby the river and then disappearing into thin air. This legend was more often told as a warning both to adults to remain faithful to their partners and to children to scare them into listening to their parents lest *La Llorona* appear in order to steal them away.

Lessons For All: Think before you act. Once you do something, it can never be undone.

Lessons For Adults: Fidelity, honor your spouse, be faithful. Watch carefully over your children and do your best to keep them from harm. Do not have children if you cannot take care of them—This lesson was shared by grade seven students, and I thought it quite wise.

Lessons For Children: Obey your parents. Do not play by the riverside alone or at night. Stay close to home.

The legend of *La Llorona* is told for many different reasons; to remind adults to be faithful, to mind their children and to think before they act. The legend is also shared to scare children so that they obey their parents lest *La Llorona* come and steal them away, to teach children to not wander away from their homes at night or to play by the river alone.

El Cadejo, Shape Shifting Devil Dog from the Mestizo culture

This legend is prevalent throughout Central America; Belize, Costa Rica, Guatemala, Honduras, Mexico, Nicaragua, and El Salvador with descriptions varying from country to country and region to region.

In Belize *El Cadejo* is described as a spirit much more powerful than an ordinary dog. He has the ability to change both size and shape, morphing from a tiny black puppy into a huge hound from hell, sometimes as large as a cow. There are two *Cadejos;* the black one represents evil and the devil, and the white one represents good and hope and is often referred to as an angel. *Cadejo* symbolizes the battle between good and evil, dark and light.

The black *Cadejo* always has red eyes, his fur is sometimes described as short and bristly like that of a pig, other times as long, shaggy and matted. He usually drags a long, thick chain behind him. He has razor sharp teeth, and a stench follows him; some described it as a goat smell others as rotting flesh. He is vicious, menacing and dangerous. He usually attacks unprovoked.

The white *Cadejo* sometimes has blue eyes, his fur is generally clean and soft. He wears no chain. The white *Cadejo* is gentle and usually appears in order to protect the victim when the black *Cadejo* attacks.

Both *Cadejos* are incredibly powerful spirits; more so than any normal dog. They are able to appear out of nowhere and disappear just as quickly. The black *Cadejo* is so powerful that there is nothing a human can do to fight him. He simply cannot be killed by human hands. One's only hope is for the white *Cadejo* to appear and come to one's defense.

In Belize, the black *Cadejo* is most often seen at night near cemeteries although he can also be found near roadsides. Sometimes he serves as a warning of an impending negative event. He often appears to drunken men, warning them to change their behavior. In several stories I heard he did not harm the men, but merely appeared in order to scare them to convince them to stop drinking. If the man does not change his behavior eventually, the black *Cadejo* will attack. In other stories, I was told the black *Cadejo* was never mindful and always attacked completely unprovoked.

My own experience with *El Cadejo*

While staying out in Bullet Tree Falls at the Parrot Nest, a small lodge with six guest cabanas, we had our own experience with what we were told was most likely *El Cadejo*. It was three o'clock in the morning. All of a sudden, the cows across the river were frightened by something, they became restless and began mooing, the birds in the trees began squawking and the dogs were barking and upset. We heard something run—as if at a gallop—through the property, something that seemed to be quite large. The entire ruckus lasted perhaps twenty minutes. The following morning we sent out Carl and Marcus to investigate. Carl is a hunter and adept at tracking. They checked the entire property and did not see a single paw print, which was quite odd as it had rained and we were in the rain forest where the ground is usually damp. We were all shaken. All of us had heard the commotion. Naida, the housekeeper, arrived and when we explained what had happened she told us that it was *El Cadejo*, and we should all be extra careful and alert in the coming days because he foretells of bad fortune.

The children shared countless stories of *El Cadejo*, of seeing dogs that were able to transform in size. There is a prevalent fear of dogs throughout Belize, especially black dogs. After hearing these stories, I understand why. I did not hear many stories about *El Cadejo* from adults. In fact, the first *El Cadejo* story I heard was from a student from El Salvador.

When sharing stories, it is important to always be mindful of how these stories may be negatively interpreted by the different cultures with whom you are working. In Dangriga during a teacher training workshop where most of the participants were Garifuna, descendants of Carib, Arawak and West African people, anger erupted when I shared stories of *El Cadejo*. They were upset because they felt it was yet another story where being black is considered bad, evil and negative and white symbolizes good. I could understand their point, and it led to an interesting discussion of race relations that I had not anticipated. I listened and honored their feelings. I also did my best to explain that the *El Cadejo* legend is from the Mestizo culture; a people deeply affected by teachings and traditions of the Catholic Church, which is prevalent throughout most of Central America. I reiterated that the focus on good versus evil, black versus white was not intended to reflect on the color of one's skin. However, their point was valid. Be aware that stories can lead to discussions you may not anticipate.

Symbolism and Lessons of El Cadejo: *El Cadejo* is the classic representation of the battle between good and evil, heaven and hell, light versus dark and black versus white. He warns against impending negative events and serves to teach general good behavior lest he appear. *El Cadejo* also serves to warn against the dangers of over-consumption of alcohol. In fact, many of the legends I heard throughout Belize seemed to carry this theme.

Xtabai and *La Llorona* as well as *Tata Duende* all warned of the dangers of excessive drinking.

CHAPTER THREE

Explode-a-Moment—Lesson Plan

Face-to-Face With Shape Shifters and Spirits

This chapter includes a lesson plan that uses indigenous legends to teach personal narrative writing. This lesson plan will utilize an exercise in which the writer meets a legend face to face, then describes what happens next.

Why is this lesson plan so important in schools?

The world is becoming smaller as globalization expands faster each year. Our communities are more diverse than ever. Diverse communities hold a commonality: every culture and every person has a story.

Personal happiness and success depend upon our ability to understand others fully and upon our ability to make ourselves understood effectively. We have to connect fully to have our needs met in the family, in the classroom, or in the community. This seemingly simple task is complicated (more so each day, it seems), by increasing social complexity, technological change, cultural tensions, and economic pressures. How can we equip young people to meet these evolving challenges?

The diverse communities I met in Belize held a commonality—which, in truth, is universal to all countries and cultures— every culture and every person has a story. These stories can serve many functions: connecting us one to another, building bridges between peoples, dispelling stereotypes and illustrating our commonalities while honoring our diversity. The stories provide a sense of self and a sense of place within the world. They tell us how the world is interconnected.

Through story, we see each other as individuals and as human beings. No longer are we defined by our governments or man-made borders. We become aware of how similar we are. When our stories are valued, we feel valued. In Belize, I found that reclaiming and honoring the wisdom of indigenous stories, by offering a process to utilize these legends in classrooms, we went a step further.

When we instill a deeper sense of value in native legends and reawaken the knowledge of the past, we infuse the present with a sudden in-rush of immediacy and significance. Stories have a dynamic power. Stories connect individuals and communities across time—past to the present, and the present to the future.

In my experience of developing this exercise over the last eight years and presenting it not only in Belize, but in the United States and France, as well as sharing the process with university students and educators through workshops in Sweden, England,

and Ghana, I've seen first-hand how effective this lesson is in engaging students. This lesson enables them to see themselves in the material presented. *Student engagement* refers to a "student's willingness, need, desire and compulsion to participate in, and be successful in, the learning process promoting higher level thinking for enduring understanding."[3]

> Research shows engaged students perform better. [Students] who are engaged show sustained behavioral involvement in learning activities accompanied by a positive emotional tone. They select tasks at the border of their competencies, initiate action when given the opportunity, and exert intense effort and concentration in the implementation of learning tasks; they show generally positive emotions during ongoing action, including enthusiasm, optimism, curiosity, and interest.[4]

Indigenous legends teach valuable lessons which connect to curriculum; in the case of the Belizean legends they teach us to have respect for each other, nature, the environment, and the world in general. Refer back to Chapter Two for more details.

In many countries, the use of indigenous legends is even more imperative to preserve and promote a local culture that

---

3. Bomia, L., Beluzo, L., Demeester, D., Elander, K., Johnson, M., & Sheldon, B., 1997. *The Impact of Teaching Strategies on Intrinsic Motivation*. Champaign, IL: ERIC Clearinghouse on Elementary and Early Childhood Education, 294.

4. Skinner, E.A., & Belmont, M.J., 1993. "Motivation in the classroom: Reciprocal effects of teacher behavior and student engagement across the school year." *Journal of Educational Psychology*, 85(4), 572.

had often been undervalued or even taken away from the local people. In Belize, these legends had been banned from the schools for a variety of reasons. Most schools in Belize are connected to churches and several of the religions viewed the legends as a form of heresy or witchcraft. Through interviews with educators, I learned that the stories were often not valued by non-Belizeans or those in power and thus were excluded from the curriculum in schools. Our cultural stories hold great power to connect us to our past and provide a sense of identity. When these stories are taken from us, we lose some sense of self. When we utilize these stories, we provide a learning experience in which indigenous culture is valued, and a sense of self can be at least partially restored.

The Importance of Creative Expression

In this day and age of standardized testing, students also need opportunities to express themselves creatively. This writing exercise provides that opportunity.

> Creativity fosters mental growth in children by providing opportunities for trying out new ideas, and new ways of thinking and problem-solving. Creative activities help acknowledge and celebrate children's uniqueness and diversity as well as offer excellent opportunities to personalize our teaching and focus on each child.[5]

↜

---

5. http://www.pbs.org/wholechild/providers/play.html

Using Indigenous Legends to Teach Creative Writing

> ➤ Lessons can be utilized in classrooms worldwide either by teachers within the school sharing the lesson directly with their students or as a workshop to teach educators how to present the lesson.

> ➤ Lessons can be used by those wishing to replicate the project within a country where they are working to preserve and share cultural stories.

> ➤ Lessons can be used in a University setting to share the value of indigenous legends and connections to the curriculum.

> ➤ Lessons can be used in community centers to connect cultures served within the area.

> ➤ Use legendary characters, creatures and beings from the cultures prevalent in your communities or classrooms or within the country where you are working to preserve and promote indigenous culture.

Step-by-Step Lesson Plan for Classrooms or Workshops

There is great flexibility in this lesson plan and how it is presented. Generally speaking, when offered for students within the classroom, I present the lessons within two to three days time utilizing several hours or class periods per day to present information, allow time for discussion, do the actual writing and share their work. I also edit each story, correcting spelling and grammar, and ask the students to revise their work incorporating the changes made. I also encourage them to add any further details they think relevant. Stories are collected a second time for one last read-through by the facilitator. On the final day, the facilitator chooses selected examples to be shared aloud with the participants. Students are also encouraged to volunteer and share their stories.

When offered as a Teacher Training Workshop, three to four hours works well to present the basic lesson plan. Again, there is flexibility in how the material is presented. Do what works for you.

There are also many options to extend the lesson plan. Some teachers chose to use the stories for drama presentations. Others created a class book including all the stories. Others extended the lesson to art and asked students to illustrate each other's stories.

Depending on which legends you share, there are also many applications to other areas of the curriculum including Science, Social Studies, History, Civics, and Cultural Studies.

How you use this lesson plan is entirely up to you. I am only providing the framework and a jumping off point.

Application of Lesson Plan

Begin with an open discussion of the indigenous legends and characters upon which you wish to focus. These can be chosen based on the most prevalent cultures present in the classroom or community where you are presenting the lesson or based upon the country where you are presenting the lesson. There are no rules or limits on how you choose the material to present. Typically I share four or five legends through summaries of the legends and student/teacher discussion. Four or five seems to provide enough choice and not overwhelm participants with too much information.

Be open to students' and teachers' suggestions of legends to share. Be open to their ideas and descriptions of the various characters and legends too because different people may have different perspectives or details of the same tale.

Utilize whatever technology you have on hand to capture the discussion. In Belize, I usually divided the blackboard into four sections, one for each of the characters we discussed and wrote down each of the descriptors shared for each of the characters so the students could refer back to the list as they wrote their introductory paragraph. You could just as easily use a flip chart, overhead projector, or smart board.

It is important to honor every answer or suggestion shared by participants in the workshop. Legends vary region-to-region and country-to-country, they even vary from village to village; therefore, a character's description may vary widely depending where the legend was heard. I have found that this validation encourages further discussion and even opens up debate among participants. It can be a wonderful learning experience and teaching tool both for the students and the educators as they share the different details they've heard. This can also lead to a discussion of how the legendary characters may be found as variations in other cultures, which leads to a discussion of how stories connect across cultures. This can be especially powerful if you have cultures in conflict within your group.

〜

Sample Script Framework for Guided Discussion—Insert your country, culture, region of choice as needed.

Facilitator: Stories are powerful, whether a legend or a folktale, a true story or a myth, our stories connect us one to another and have valuable lessons to teach us. When we know our own cultural stories we feel a sense of pride and empowerment. Your stories are important. (You may wish to elaborate and share why you are interested in their culture and stories.)

Today I'd like to open a discussion about legends here in Belize. Have any of you ever heard any of the legends from Belize? Who or what do you think is the most prominent legend in Belize?

Participants respond with several answers, all are noted and encouraged.

Facilitator: Let's begin with *Tata Duende* (I always started with him because he was the most widely known legend and generally speaking this created a flow of call/response with participants.)

Who can tell me one detail they have heard about *Tata Duende?* What does he look like? Where might you see him? What are some of his character traits from the legends you have heard?

Participants share details which I then note on the blackboard or flip chart. The discussion builds on the details shared by participants.

Note: If participants are more reserved, ask prompting

questions or provide a few details to get them started. It is important that you share legends and characters you have thoroughly researched so you have a grasp of the material. It is also important to be flexible and to accept details you may have not heard previously.

Facilitator: What does *Tata Duende* do? Why does he live in the forest? What is *Tata Duende's* purpose? What do the legends about him teach us? What are the lessons for us to learn?

Participants respond.

Facilitator: Have any of you heard any stories about *Tata Duende?* Would you be open to sharing the stories you've heard?

Participants respond.

Facilitator: Have any of you had any personal experiences with *Tata Duende?*

Participants respond.

Facilitator: Do you think *Tata Duende* was or is a real person? (This leads to fascinating discussions about how at times legends arise out of real events, situations, circumstances, or people and are exaggerated over time to become perhaps a bit more fanciful.)

Participants respond.

Note: We connect the legends to real life experiences and share how and why they are perhaps based on real events. In my opinion, this shows an even deeper respect for the culture and stories.

Facilitator: What is the symbolism in the *Tata Duende* legend? What might be the deeper layers of the story?

Notes: With each legend, we discuss how the story has been and can be used to speak about difficult or taboo topics. The story allows listeners and tellers to share subjects they might not otherwise feel comfortable speaking about. The story allowed the common man to speak more openly about those in power, whether another culture or a government. This concept is directly connected to the legends presented by asking participants to identify how the legends being discussed are connected to difficult subjects and encouraging further conversation about those issues.

Allow thirty to forty minutes for the discussion of legends and characters. Thank participants for their suggestions and being open and willing to discuss.

The following is a list of suggestions of legends that have been successfully shared from other cultures:

> Big Foot: USA, Canada
> *Chupacabra*: Dominican Republic, Argentina, Bolivia, Chile, Colombia, Honduras, El Salvador, Nicaragua, Panama, Peru, Brazil, United States, and Mexico
> Dragons: Worldwide
> Fate/Fairy: Italy, Ireland, across Europe
> Horned Serpent/Uktena: Native American
> Loch Ness Monster: Scotland
> Pooka: Ireland
> *Smok Waweski*: Poland
> Underwater Panther: Native American (Algonquin)
> Yeti: Nepal, Tibet (similar to Big Foot)

Introduce the Writing Experience/Exercise

Keep it simple. Especially when working with English as a Second Language or Foreign Language students. Generally speaking, this writing exercise is two to three paragraphs:

> An introductory paragraph describing the character and setting in detail,

> A paragraph in which the student meets the character face-to-face and utilizes the Explode-a-Moment technique, a moment-by-moment description of the action.

The writing exercise is presented with the use of storytelling to share examples of stories already written by other students. The Facilitator might also tell stories impromptu about various legendary figures (if the presenter feels comfortable doing so.)

Script of Detailed Step-by-Step Instruction of the Lesson

Note: this is one example of a lesson plan or script. You are welcome to modify as you see fit, to change any of the content as it suits you best. This is simply a place to start.

Facilitator: Now it's time to write! (Say this with great enthusiasm!)

Each of you will choose one of the legendary characters we just discussed, and I will guide you in writing your own short story about what would happen if you met that legend face-to-face! Can you imagine meeting *La Llorona* or *El Cadejo*? What would happen? How would you feel? Would you invite her in for a cup of tea? Would you reach out and pet *El Cadejo*? (I try to inject some humor here to loosen up participants.)

Please take a moment and choose the character about whom you'd like to write your short story. Please select the character you think and feel you can best describe. (Give students two to five minutes to choose.)

Please write the legend's name at the top of your paper. Has everyone chosen a legend? Excellent!

We will use all of our senses in the story and will write it like a short movie; we will create images for our readers like photographs or paintings out of our descriptive words.

Please listen carefully as I provide the framework for the story. We will write on every other line of the paper so that correcting and editing is easier. Take a moment and make an X in the margin of every other line down the side of your paper. When you write, only write on the lines with an X. (Show them on the blackboard.)

First, let me share an example of a few of the stories written by students here in Belize. (Choose a few stories from Chapter Four and read out loud to provide a sense of the writing exercise).

Let's begin with a short introductory paragraph. What do we need to share with the reader in our introductory paragraph?

Participants almost always respond with, "Main character and setting."

Facilitator: Yes, the main character and setting. (I usually provide the first sentence of the story because this is where many of the students became stuck. When using this as teacher training, I give the option of using a standardized first sentence or creating their own.)

Facilitator: Let's begin with the following sentence: In the village (city) of _____ (you choose whichever village or city you would like the story to take place in—and yes, it needs to be a real place) there lives _____. (Insert the name of the legend you have chosen to write about.)

Note: When working with students whose English and grammar are very basic, we even speak about what type of letter a sentence begins with (a Capital) and that a sentence ends with (a period or full-stop). I write an example of an extremely long, mistake-ridden run-on sentence on the board and ask students to help fix it.

Example:

this da story bout *Tata Duende* a wee short tiny miniature man with backway feets who live in da bush wit animals like the deer and then gibnut and the jaguar and all the trees the Ceiba the pine the palm and he whistle and he play da guitar and he like to play trick on you and he thief childrens and he plait horse hair and he play marble

Note: Before they begin writing their introductory paragraph, share examples of strong writing. You are welcome to share some of the introductory paragraphs from the students' and teachers' stories included in this book. It helps participants to hear the format before they begin themselves.

Facilitator: Before we begin our paragraphs let's first talk about *strong word choice*. Strong word choice does not mean using a lot of big, fancy or unusual words. Mostly, it means using the right word to say the right thing in just the right way.

Additionally, it may mean using active verbs (scampered) rather than common or dull verbs (ran). It means thinking before you write and perhaps sounding it out in your head. Let's do a participatory word game to get our creative juices flowing.

Participatory Exercise: Strong Adjective/Noun Word Choice.

Facilitator: Which description grabs your attention?

> *Tata Duende* is a small man wearing a huge hat. He has twisted backward feet and lives in the forest.

> *Tata Duende*, a diminutive man, wears a sombrero so large it practically covers his eyes. His deformed legs twist backward so that his feet perpetually point in the wrong direction. He dwells under the lush canopy of Ceiba trees.

The second description *shows* rather than *tells*. It is specific, you can see *Tata Duende*, you can see the Ceiba trees. When we show rather than tell, we help our reader or listener to create pictures in their own minds so they can more clearly follow our story.

Notes: Lead a discussion about strong adjectives by writing examples of weak adjectives on the board and then asking for suggestions of stronger replacements. Write those suggestions on the board. Encourage words that show rather than tell. Weak words include small, big, nice, good, long, dirty, kind, mean, mad, etc. A list of strong adjectives is included in Appendices at the end of the book.

Option: Divide the class into smaller groups of three to five students and give each group a short sentence with a weak word. Ask the groups to re-write the sentences using stronger word choices. Share the results with the class.

Examples of strong student writing:

Thick razor teeth protruded from his gaping mouth.
—Amira Bol, BMRC, age twelve.

He was sly, tricky, conniving, quick with his wrong-doing.
—Justin Chun, BMRC, age eleven.

Tata Duende is a clever, quick-tempered, lonely man.
—Ebony Cornish, St. Joseph School, age ten.

Facilitator: Excellent job on the strong word exercise. Now that our creative juices are flowing, please add three to seven sentences describing the main character and setting to your introductory paragraph. What does he/she look like? What is he/she wearing? What are some of the common actions of this character? Setting: please describe the setting. Where does this character live? What does the location look like? Remember to paint a picture with words and to be specific with your word choices.

Run-on Exercise

Facilitator: Let's be mindful of run-on sentences and spelling. Here's an example of an actual sentence, just as a student wrote it. (Write this on the blackboard, flipchart or smart board.) Let's edit this together:

> *Tata Duende* is one small little man with his feet twisted backway and he wheres a big huge tall hat

and he lives in the forest with all the animals and plants and he protects them from being over hunted or from too many trees cut down and he loves to play guitar even tho he has no tumbs wich is very strang but they say he wistles loud and he is near and soft and he is far and he likes the color red and he lives in bullet tree falls village where he likes to play tricks on the people

Notes: Allow fifteen to twenty minutes for the strong word and run-on sentence exercises. Allow ten to fifteen minutes for writing the first paragraph. Timing depends on your students' abilities.

Check for understanding as participants are writing about the Main Character and Setting. I usually walk around the room and look at their writing to be sure they are following directions and to offer support. At the end of decided time allotment ask if anyone is willing to share his/her introductory paragraph with the class. I also usually choose two or three students to share based on the writing I witnessed as I walked around the room.

Facilitator: Who would like to read their introductory paragraph? Thank you for your courage! Hearing other people's creativity can provide inspiration for others. Please stand and read it loudly so we can hear.

Big applause afterwards!

Explode-a-Moment—Second Paragraph

Explode-a-Moment is an exercise in creating a movie with words; the writer shares a moment-by-moment, second-by-second description of action using all five senses.

Facilitator: Now the real fun begins. Imagine meeting this character face to face. Imagine what would happen next.

We will use a writing technique called Explode-a-Moment. In this technique you will create a sort of movie with words. You will write a moment-by-moment, second-by-second description of the action as it happens. Use all five senses. What are the five senses?

Participants respond: Seeing, Hearing, Touching, Smelling, Tasting

Facilitator: In Explode-a-Moment you also share "thought-shots," what you were thinking/feeling as the action happens. The action takes place in a very short period of time; imagine the next five to ten, fifteen or twenty minutes with this character. Writing with Explode-a-Moment keeps the action and story very focused. Explode-a-Moment enhances your writing; it stretches out the moment as if it is occurring in slow motion. Start with the very first action that takes place when you see the legend face-to-face. Then build from there, following in sequence moment-by-moment what you are seeing, hearing, feeling, smelling, touching or tasting.

Before we leap into writing the Explode-a-Moment paragraph, let's do another Participatory Exercise.

Strong Verb Choices Exercise

Facilitator: What is a verb?

Participants: Verbs are action words.

Facilitator: Correct, verbs are words that describe the

action in a sentence. Some are stronger than others and will make your writing more interesting. Strong verbs show instead of tell. The writer creates a mental picture by using words that are specific or concrete (as in visual or otherwise expressive of the five senses).

Compare these two sentences:

➤   He ran to the tree.

➤   He sprinted to the tree.

Which sentence tells you more? Yes, the second one. It tells you how he ran. (On the board, write the word Run.)

Facilitator: What are some other words for "run" that give us more detail? What words might tell us how one was running?

Participants share other word choices:

➤   Sprint

➤   Jog

➤   Dash

➤   Flee, etc.

(Write their answers on the board.)

Facilitator: Let's do the same with each of the following words:

➤   Walk

➤   Look

➤   Went

➤   Ate

➤   Get

➤   Said

〜

Small Group Strong Verb Exercise

Divide the class into five or six groups. Give each group one of the following sentences written on a piece of paper:

> I saw a dog.
> He looked at me.
> I walked down the street.
> He ate the apple.

Notes: Ask the students to rewrite the sentences using stronger verb choices. You can also ask them to elaborate and add adjectives and strong nouns. Encourage them to show rather than tell, to create a mental picture. Ask the students to share their rewritten sentences. Thank them for their suggestions.

Facilitator: Here are a couple of favorite examples of strong word choices from Belizean students:

The diabolical beast leaped on me and dragged me
down the road.
—Valentin Vanejos BMRC, grade six.

Defiantly walking, I contemplated whether I should
go back to the river or return home and apologize
for my behavior.
—Laura Ramos, BMRC, age twelve.

Similes and Metaphors Exercise

Facilitator: Similes and Metaphors also add flavor to your writing. What is a simile?

Participants respond: Responses will vary so you may want to affirm correct parts of responses and then assert the desired definition …

Facilitator: Yes, a simile compares two unlike things using like or as.

Here are some favorite student responses from Belize:

She was grey like the clouds when it wanted to rain.
—Holly Palacio St. Ignatious, age twelve.

He stared at me as if he knew me. His face, big, wrinkled, fat like a balloon full of air ready to burst.
—Andy Quiroz, BMRC, age eleven.

His anger exploded like a volcano.
—Jhurdy Marroquin, BMRC, age eleven.

Note: At this point, I almost always allow students to share a few similes.

Facilitator: What is a metaphor?

Participants respond.

Facilitator: Yes, a metaphor is a comparison of unlike things. Or a situation is compared to a real thing. No "like" or "as" is used.

> ➤ It was raining cats and dogs.
> ➤ She has a bubbly personality.
> ➤ He was fishing for a compliment.

Facilitator: Let's Write! (At this point, you may allow participants to choose their own beginning, or you might prefer to proceed to the next exercise.)

Explode-a-Moment Writing Exercise

This is an exercise to help students begin paragraph two.

I have found the prompt to be helpful in guiding the writing. Please remind participants that in this particular exercise there are only two characters in the story: the legendary character chosen and themselves. This also keeps the writing focused. Some students do choose to add a parent or a friend. But definitely, keep it to only one legendary character.

However, if you are working with advanced writers, then it might be great fun to depart from the "one legendary character" rule. Advanced writers would be up to the challenge of having multiple legends meet and interact with each other. But that is another lesson for another time.

Facilitator: The second paragraph beings with the following sentence:

One night while I was_____ (insert any activity you like here, the more descriptive the better. For example, not paying attention to my little brother, outside picking a bouquet of flowers for my mother or in my room reading a horror novel by Stephen King.) I met _____ (insert the name of the legendary character about whom you are writing) and after that, my life was never the same. (This last part is optional, but it adds some umph!)

Here are some of my favorite Belizean student writing examples from this exercise:

> One night while I was camping in the woods I met
> *El Cadejo.* I had just returned from fetching water
> at the river when I noticed a figure staring at me
> through the bushes.
> —Ebony Cornish St. Joseph RC School, grade six.

One night when I went to the waterfall to bathe, I noticed a lady at the top of the waterfall crying and singing into her empty folded hands as if a baby was in them.
—Stephanie Windsor, grade seven.

One night when I was supposed to be doing my homework, I went into the forbidden cave and believe me it wasn't called the forbidden cave because it smelled like flowers. No, it was the home of *Tata Duende*.
—Kevin Singh, St. Joseph School, grade seven.

Facilitator: Students, please spend the next two minutes writing the first sentence of your Explode-a-Moment paragraph.

Facilitator: Now that you have a first sentence, let's take a moment before continuing to write. Close your eyes and see the character standing right in front of you. How does your body react? Do you look them in the eye? Do your eyes widen in fear? How do you feel? Are you frightened or perhaps excited? Are you shaking? Is your heart beating faster? How do your legs feel? What do you smell? What sounds do you hear? (Allow three to five minutes with eyes closed to picture the action unfolding.)

Discussion: What did you see in your mind as you imagined meeting the character face-to-face? Think about what the character might do upon meeting you. How do they react to you? What do they do? What do they say?

Participants may share a few examples of what they saw in their mind's eye.

Notes: Share some examples of Explode-a-Moment. You

are welcome to use the student and teacher stories within this book. If you wish and enjoy telling stories, you can spin a story live. Never fear the impromptu. I always do this step because I love to share dramatic, theatrical stories.

The story does not need to be negative. It could, in fact, lead to an interesting encounter. Several students have written of how they became friends with *Tata Duende* and helped him utilize his powers for good rather than being a troublesome trickster.

Allow thirty minutes for the description of Explode-a-Moment and the Participatory Exercises.

Allow participants to write for thirty to forty-five minutes depending if they are students or teachers. Check in with them periodically, either as a group or walk around the room and check in on their progress individually.

Editing and Revising

Editing and revising is always included in the student lesson plan. I briefly explain the process to the teachers in the workshop setting.

Facilitator: Rarely is a story finished in the very first draft. Editing and revising is an essential part of the process. Take a moment to quietly and slowly read your story out loud to be sure everything in your head made it onto the paper. When we read something slowly and out loud we can often hear mistakes we might not otherwise notice. Check your own spelling and grammar. Check to be sure your subjects and verbs agree. As a second step, if you wish, exchange your stories with one another and check for spelling and grammatical errors. Another pair of eyes is always helpful to find things we may not catch. (Allow ten minutes for final editing before collecting the first draft of the stories.)

Collect Stories

Facilitator: Thank you for sharing your creativity today. I look forward to reading your stories.

Notes: When I offer this workshop directly for students, I collect all the stories and edit them, correcting spelling and grammar and writing specific notes for improvement on each student's story.

Day One complete, total time is between ninety minutes and two hours for Students. You can take longer if needed, it is entirely up to you—and to the ability of the students you are teaching.

Teacher Workshop: Day One, Two and Three are combined into one three to four hour session.

Night of Day One:

Facilitator edits and corrects stories. I choose to be very detailed in my corrections, not simply circling errors, but making the actual spelling and grammatical corrections so the students can see the changes. I also include suggestions for improving the story, "insert transition here" or "please describe more how you felt when *Tata Duende* leaped through your window." "Excellent start, please tell us what happened next after you ran outside. What did you do? What did *Tata Duende* do?" "Please keep the action focused in five to ten minutes time." "Your ending seems very abrupt, please add three or four more sentences of action before you end the story."

The more detail you provide in your feedback for the students, the better their revisions or second drafts will be. I never correct using a red pen. It looks like blood to me. Choose purple or blue or green. Anything, but red. Thanks!

Day Two—Revising, Second Draft

Student lesson plan includes the following:

> ➤ Return the corrected stories, highlighting some of the best writing and providing positive feedback as well as what can be improved for each student.
> ➤ Group editing exercise.
> ➤ Provide time for re-write.
> ➤ Share examples of excellent writing.
> ➤ Share positive feedback and general improvement notes for all participants.

Facilitator: Thank you so much for sharing your creativity in your stories. There were so many excellent Explode-a-Moment descriptions. First, I want to highlight a few sentences I really enjoyed and then I'd like to share some positive feedback. Finally, let's talk about where the writing can be improved.

Edit Sentences: Write a few sentences on the blackboard from the writing of the students. Students who wrote the sentences are not identified. Usually, I combine several mistakes into one sentence. As a group, we correct the mistakes. This is always quite powerful.

Facilitator: Let's edit a few sentences together. See if you can find the mistakes in spelling and grammar.

Example of sentence to edit, write on the blackboard, flip chart or smartboard:

> one night wile I was doing my homework I herd a loud noise behind me so I turn around and der was Tata Duende staring at me wit his big ugle face looking at me in my eyes so I try to scrim but I cannot and then my brodder hear me and he come running in my room and he say what is wrong why you scriming so loud so I tell him look there is Tata Duende right there at the windo and he scrim to Tata Duende jump in the windo at us he have a big machete an he chop my brodder tumb of and I scrim more loud and my dad come running and he say what is going on and I point at Tata Duende and my brodder and then I faint

Notes: In Belize nearly every student is speaking and writing English as a Second Language, making the spelling and grammar more of a challenge. However, they are excellent at spotting mistakes and correcting them. This exercise makes them feel successful.

I always express the challenge of writing in a language that is not one's first language and compliment them on everything they have done well. I highlight the creativity present, telling students how I feel that creativity is a gift that often cannot be taught. Spelling and grammar can be learned.

Allow twenty minutes for sharing excellent writing examples, editing sentences together and returning stories to each student.

Facilitator: Let's now work on the revision or your second draft. Rarely is a writer finished in one or even two rewriting sessions. They edit, revise, rewrite. We will do this together today.

Please take out another blank sheet of paper. Please carefully re-write your story, paying close attention to the corrections made and suggestions and questions for improving the story. Think about how you can show your reader everything that happened moment by moment with words. Once again quietly read your story out loud to yourself. Listen to hear where there may be areas you can add details to Explode-a-Moment. Was anything missing in your first draft? Did you keep to the moment-by-moment description? Does it make sense? If you have any questions about the corrections, suggestions or ideas for improving the story, please ask me. I will come to each one of you individually as you write and revise.

Notes:
- ➤ Allow thirty to forty minutes for re-writing.
- ➤ Check in with each student for understanding of corrections, suggestions or ideas for improving their stories.
- ➤ At the end of the session ask students to exchange their revised stories with each other and check each other's writing.
- ➤ Ask students to quietly read their own stories out loud checking for mistakes.
- ➤ Allow sixty to ninety minutes for Day Two Exercises and Re-Write.
- ➤ Collect revisions.

Facilitator: Thank you for taking the time to revise and rewrite your stories including the corrections and suggestions for improvement. Thank you for respecting yourselves enough to do your best work. I will edit and correct your revisions, your second drafts and return them tomorrow. I will choose the five or six best stories to be read in front of the class for the rest of the students. I will also ask for two or three other volunteers who would like to share their stories.

Day Three: Sharing Participant Stories

Facilitator: I enjoyed reading your revisions. Thank you for including the corrections and for being respectful of yourselves to add the requested suggestions for improvement. I was honored reading your work. The best part has come, you sharing your work for the rest of the participants.

It is difficult to choose the best, but some of the stories definitely grabbed my attention, were super creative and had an extra level of wonder! I would like to ask five of you to share your stories in front of the class. Please read your story loudly so we all can hear. Stand tall. Be proud of the work you created. Respect yourself, your work and each other. After these five students have shared their stories I will ask for three or four more volunteers to share their stories. Please let us all be respectful of one another and listen attentively.

Notes:
> Students share stories.
> Volunteers share stories.
> Allow thirty to forty-five minutes for sharing. You

can also extend this activity and have everyone share their work, how you do this final exercise is entirely up to you.

> I make photocopies or ask students to copy the five best stories, and I keep them.

Teacher-Training Time Frame:

If you are offering this exercise as a Teacher-Training Workshop the time frame is generally:

> Five to ten minutes for introduction of self and importance of storytelling.
> Ten minutes to explain application of lesson to classroom setting.
> Twenty to thirty minutes for discussion of legends.
> Fifteen to twenty minutes for explanation of introductory paragraph and participatory exercises.
> Fifteen minutes for writing introductory paragraph.
> Ten to fifteen minutes break.
> Thirty minutes for explanation of Explode-a-Moment and participatory exercises.
> Thirty minutes for writing Explode-a-Moment paragraph.
> Five to ten minutes for editing and revisions.
> Twenty minutes for sharing stories.
> Ten minutes for questions.
> Five to seven minutes for evaluations.
> Total time: approximately three to four hours.

You can view the entire training sequence on my YouTube channel, storytellerkp:

https://www.youtube.com/playlist?list=PL288E81D9A2C12315

Extending the Exercise

This creative writing exercise can be extended far beyond a three-day participatory workshop. Educators and storytellers are welcome to utilize this lesson as a jumping off point for theatrical presentations, class books of stories, connection to other areas of the curriculum such as social sciences, environmental sciences, history, civics. The possibilities are endless and only limited by imagination.

Students excited to share their work at St. Joseph Roman
Catholic School, Belize City, grade three.

Enthused after storytelling at Bishop Martin Roman
Catholic School, San Ignacio, grade one.

Children excited to receive book donations at La Immaculata School in Bullet Tree Falls.

Nursery students peruse donated books at St. Joseph Roman Catholic School in Belize City.

My sanctuary at the Parrot Nest in Bullet Tree Falls. Thanks to Theo Cocchi.

Grade five and six students react to receiving book
donations at La Immaculata School in Bullet Falls.

Students participate in a Story at Bishop Martin Roman Catholic School in San

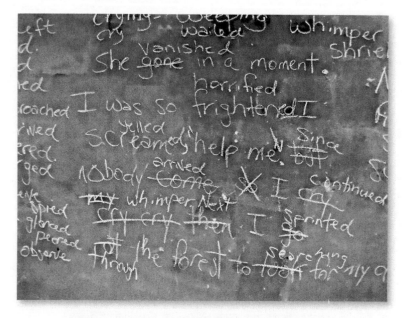

Editing sentences at Bishop Martin Roman Catholic School
in San Ignacio as part of creative writing workshop.

Guadalupe Roman Catholic School.

My sanctuary at the Parrot Nest in Bullet Tree Falls. Thanks to Theo Cocchi.

Teacher Training Session at Sacred Heart in San Ignacio.

Tall trees at Caves Branch with Robin Reichert from the US.

This is a typical village school, La Immaculata School, Bullet Tree Falls.

The Belize bus system comprised of used school buses from the US.

This is the route I walked home each day from Bishop Martin Roman Catholic School in San Ignacio to Parrot Nest in Bullet Tree Falls.

Sharing stories at a Maya School in Toledo District, Southern Belize. These children had never seen a white person before.

CHAPTER FOUR

Student and Teacher Stories

[Editor's note: The example stories appear here unedited, so that the reader may understand the level of response received in these actual in-school exercises.]

Most of the following stories were written by students from upper primary school, grades six and seven. School names are indicated when they are known. Please keep in mind that all of these students speak English as their second or even third language. These stories are the best of the hundreds of stories written by the students for whom I was fortunate to present workshops. The teacher stories are the few that were shared from the teacher training workshops. Note: these stories were edited during the workshops. However they contain the final product as presented by the students or teachers. I was highly impressed with their use of language, intense imagery, and deep creativity. Multiple stories about each legend are presented.

⌐

El Cadejo

Jurel Valdez, Grade Seven

In the village of The Valley of Peace there lives *El Cadejo*. The ferocious beasts duel in the cemetery. They come out at night in search of mortals. They are black and white, the black one is unholy and protects people from being devoured alive. They battle each other so the winner can do anything in his leisure. Black *Cadejo* is a shape shifter; the more you fear him, the more powerful he gets. Black *Cadejo* has red eyes that paralyze people with fear. He has claws that can shred people into pieces. His tail is like a razor sharp blade to slice his prey in half. Never pet Cadejo.

One night I was while I was taking out the garbage I met Black *Cadejo*. I noticed red eyes like a great white shark ready to devour me. I wailed at him. He sprinted towards me faster than lightning. The creature tried to bite my foot, but I kicked him in the head. His head was twisted all the way around slowly I heard bones cracking. It was trying to put its head back together. Then suddenly I saw a flash of light appear. It was White *Cadejo*. They were scratching and biting each other. I got frightened I noticed Black *Cadejo* nails grow longer and his jaw expanded. I prayed and White *Cadejo* grew enormous. With his giant jaw he bit and swung Black *Cadejo* like a toy and threw him into a tree. He got up but with a mighty slash the Black *Cadejo* disintegrated, but I knew it wasn't dead. White *Cadejo* told me, it didn't move its mouth, but I heard its voice in my head. It continued and said, "After I depart from here you will never see Black *Cadejo* again." He left in a bolt of lightning, and I never saw them again, but I am still safe from Black *Cadejo*.

⸂

**Ivan Hernandez, Grade Six,
Bishop Martin RC School**

In the village of *Santa Familia* there live the *Cadejos*. They are the largest of all dogs with the ugliest of faces. There are two *Cadejos*, at least that's what I've heard. The white one signifies love and peace, on the other hand the black one with red fiery eyes that burn like the fires of hell signifies the demons and all things that are bad. They are said to be found in many places, but I met these two in the unforgiving forest.

One night while I was camping I met the evil *Cadejo* feeding on what looked like a baby deer. His red and gruesome looking eyes staring right at me like an irritated bull ready to charge. I was scared to death of this horrible sight. In the blink of an eye it arose from its meal and came walking slowly towards the troop of campers and me. I was shaking with fear as it growled at us. I knew we couldn't run because it would catch us for sure. During this mind blowing suspense out of nowhere another colossal dog galloped towards us and stood bravely in front of us. He was growling ferociously at the Black *Cadejo*. When I saw the expressions on their faces, I knew the battle was about to begin. Suddenly, a dark mist shrouded the Black *Cadejo* as it sprinted towards us; somehow the White *Cadejo* followed him. The Black *Cadejo* drew back his huge paw and hit the White *Cadejo* with all his might. The White *Cadejo* went flying through the air. There was an all-out battle between good and evil right before our eyes. The mist intoxicated the White *Cadejo* and it landed right in front of me. I could not believe my ears when suddenly I heard it whisper to me. "You must pray to help me win this battle." I told the troop to start praying to help the White *Cadejo*. They all did, it seemed to give him strength. Finally, the White *Cadejo* arose and gave the Black *Cadejo* an all out smack down! Pow! Thump!

Crash! We couldn't believe our eyes.

The sun started to rise and I noticed that the *Cadejos* were fading away, in the hazy light we could still see them fighting. To this day I believe they are still at war even though the scene I witnessed was over five years ago.

‽

Ymir Zuniga, Grade Six, Bishop Martin Roman Catholic School

In the village of Duck Run II there lives *el Cadejo*. How do you I know you ask? Unfortunately, I met one. It was the most vicious and evil animal I had ever seen. With eyes as red as blood, fur as dark as the night with no moon. *Caedejo* has the amazing ability of changing forms and growing to immense sizes. Most of the time he is found in a graveyard, but also can be seen on dark streets. With luck rather than see a black *Cadejo*, you will see a white one. This one has fur as white as snow and is as kind as a rabbit.

One night I was walking down the dark road when I caught a glimpse of two huge red eyes staring right at me. In my fear I tried to run, but I stumbled. I could hear the loud pounding of his feet right behind me. I tried to see what was coming up behind me but it was no use as its fur was as black as the night which surrounded us. I saw nothing. Unfortunately, I fell to the ground with a thump, as I turned around the shimmer from the moon shown on what had been chasing me. I thought I was about to meet my end as a snarling face came right at me. Luckily, I had a machete in my hand. I swung with all my might, just hard enough to harm the beast. With *el Cadejo* distracted, I dashed away.

With just enough speed, I ran back home with sweat running down my back like rain on a stormy night. My mom asked me what happened but I couldn't speak from the fear I'd had. I never saw him again.

⤳

James Sierra, Grade Seven

In the village of San Felipe there lives *El Cadejo*. They say he comes out at night to look for drunken men or children who disobey their parents or children who are out playing on the streets late at night. His eyes as red as blood, his body is as bony as a half dissolved decaying dog that just rose out of his death slumber. His remaining fur is as black as a moonless night. You may be the wimpiest or bravest kid, but even you can be afraid of the *El Cadejo*.

One windy chilly night we were on our way to a village named San Felipe. We were going to visit family members who we hadn't seen in a long while. We stayed at our cousin's house that night. He told us there were two missing children and it was discovered they were killed by someone or something. People believe it was the *El Cadejo* but no one has proof. On that night while I was sleeping I heard something calling my name, "James, James!" As curious as I am, I went outside. San Felipe is a dark place, there is not much light in the village. The voice lured me to a farm not too far away from my cousin's house, perhaps three-fourths of a mile away. There in the distance red eyes, I didn't know what it was. Then all of a sudden all the animals nearby started to make noise. The cows were mooing, dogs barking, chickens clucking, even the rooster was making a fuss. And then a loud "boom!" Afterwards everything went quiet. I was now terrified. "How can there be thunder on a clear night?" Then it hit me. I thought perhaps it was the *chubacabra*, an animal that feeds on flesh. But I was mistaken. *El Cadejo* pounced on me. I fell with a hard thud. I closed my eyes, when I opened them I saw huge fangs drooling with blood right in my face. His breath was disgusting. Then a white light shone on me. *El Cadejo* quickly moved away. I saw a white dog and I thought for sure I was going crazy. They stood facing each other. In the blink of an eye they both collided, the earth shook with a sound like thunder; it was as if the sky had opened to a tremendous storm. I felt like running, but the fight was too awesome to behold. I couldn't leave. Boom! Pow! Boom! They were moving faster than light. "No, I will Not be beaten like this!" said the Black *Cadejo* vanishing into thin air. The White *Cadejo* approached me and said, "you've handled yourself well."

After that I fainted. I woke up in bed and asked myself, was it all a dream?

⤳

John Harrison, Grade Six

In the village of San Jose, there lives an evil dog named *El Cadejo*. *El Cadejo* has black fur, evil red eyes, horns on his head and a bull's tail. This folklore character usually attacks people who are walking down the road alone late at night. The second *Cadejo* is a bright white furred dog which protects people from the Black *Cadejo*. It usually appears when the Black *Cadejo* attacks innocent people, chasing the Black *Cadejo* away.

One night while my brother and I were playing monopoly we heard chains rattling out in the street. We peeped through the window to see what was making so much noise. When we saw it was a black dog we thought it was our dog. We went out into the dark freezing night to search for another chain to tie the dark dog down. As soon as my brother ran to get the other chain from the shed, I dashed to grab the dog. When I called the dog's name it turned around. Then I saw the dog's blood red eyes, I knew immediately it wasn't ours. I stepped back a few feet. As it stared at me with those bloody red eyes, I knew I was toast.

My heart was beating faster than a drummer drumming, my legs turned to jelly and I couldn't move. Suddenly, something as bright as the sun appeared in front of me. It pushed me and the feeling came back to my legs. I stepped back and bolted away from the battlefield. When I turned around I saw a colossal fist force the Black *Cadejo* back into the underworld. I went back into my house to find my brother. He was inside. I was glad everyone was safe. From then on, I hoped to never encounter the Black *Cadejo* again.

〜

The next story is included to illustrate comparison of writing from primary to high school. Only sixty percent of students who take the PSE, national exam to enter high school, pass. Thus, only talented students get into high school.

**Tarun Butche, Grade Ten,
Sacred Heart Junior College**

Wind blowing and thunder blaring, rain pelted the zinc roof of our four room wooden house nestled among the leaf littered forest floor. Opening my eyes and staring at the dark and seemingly endless ceiling, sweat beaded on the corners of my forehead lazily rolling down my fiery cheeks. I caught a glimpse out of the corner of my eyes, humongous flaring scarlet eyes starting right at me. Instantly, I realized it was *El Cadejo*.

Fear filled my body, my blood turning to ice. My trembling, almost paralyzed fingers gripped the comforter as I pulled it over my head to completely shield my face from the terrifying beast. I could hear a slight growl escape his clenched saw-like teeth. Thud! Thud! His paws lifting up and down, hitting the floor like a small tremor, the sound penetrating my ears. I peeked from under my sheets, my bottom lip quivered at the sight of the enormous creature. "It won't notice me if I lie here still as a dead possum," I cried to myself. But before I could react a loud cry escaped my lips. In less than the blink of an eye he was over me. His weight too heavy for my small bed and with a Crash! It hit the floor. It's saliva dripping off his fanged teeth onto my face. As I closed my eyes and prayed to be out of the horrible situation, I wake awoken from my fear, by his tongue licking my face. Impossible! Despicable! I was terrified on what was my own Pomeranian puppy!

☙

Xtabai

Next, the best primary school writer I encountered in Belize. He was only twelve when he wrote the following story.

Joshua Parham, Grade Seven,
St. Joseph RC School, Belize City

There is a legend that lives all over the country of Belize, but is mostly found in the village of St. Ann's. They say there was once a woman who lived in an uncharted village. She was very beautiful; she had long rich black hair, smooth clear skin and green eyes with a jovial mood. But something had scarred her forever. They say her spirit still lives and at night she becomes the most terrifying creature with scaly skin, goat legs and a hunched back. They call her *Xtabai*.

I am not the type of person to believe in legends; I don't have the time, but a mysterious event changed all that. It was in the year 2011, February 1. I was just sitting at home; which was weird because I normally have a busy schedule. Then the telephone rang, it was my best friend *Jakaki*, he was excited. *Jakaki* wanted to go to a party in St. Ann's which is now the name of the uncharted village where *Xtabai* lived. It is funny how quickly the day went by because before I knew it we were at the party in St. Ann's. We were having a blast, it was the time of my life. *Jakaki* was already intoxicated and vomiting, so I advised him to take himself outside. I was dancing and oddly, my feet felt as if they had no weight. I wasn't thinking about yesterday or tomorrow. Someone started to smoke a substance with nicotine. I am very sensitive to nicotine so I went outside. I still had all my five senses because I hadn't touched anything with alcohol. I couldn't say the same for *Jakaki*.

Then I saw him, smiling and walking into the forest. I was curious about what he was doing so I silently followed behind. *Jakaki* was walking on a trail that went deep into the forest. At first I thought he lost something, but I saw him smiling. He was mesmerized by something. It was a girl, a very beautiful and sexy girl in her early twenties. I looked at her closely, she had clear skin, green eyes and long rich black hair. Could it be?! No! Yes! It was the *Xtabai!* I felt a chill go down my spine. I feared for *Jakaki's* life but also for my own. I had no idea what to do. Should I evade her and save my own life or should I put myself in harm's way to save *Jakaki's* life? I chose loyalty over safety and yelled, *"Jakaki!* She's *Xtabai!"* *Jakaki* gave a slurred reply which I couldn't understand. He then spun around and fell face first on the ground. The beautiful dame began her transformation into the hideous beast with backwards feet, hunched back and scaly skin. Her eyes became full black and her once sweet gentle voice became heavy and deep. She bellowed, "Who's that? Get away! Or you will be next!"

My heart began to race and then I began to sweat. Adrenaline was injected into me. I remembered the stories. The stories said that if *Xtabai* sees a cross she must leave the area. I had to think fast because she was already slowly pulling *Jakaki* into her enormous cave. I quickly broke off two twigs from a tree which I was hiding behind. I bended the twigs to form the shape of a cross and pointed it towards *Xtabai*. She shrieked, "AAAAHHHHH!" as she vanished into thin air. I quickly dashed to *Jakaki*. I asked, "Dude, are you all right?!" There was no response. "Could he be dead?" I thought to myself. I didn't remember if she had done anything to him that was possibly lethal. I became apprehensive. I checked his pulse, it was still beating. I then put my finger under his nose and discovered he was still breathing. I breathed a sigh of relief. He was just wasted; totally out of it.

The night was very dark and we were deep in the forest, but I could have found my way back to the house. I pulled *Jakaki* up off the ground and threw him over my shoulder and walked back to the house. When I arrived back to the house with *Jakaki* I told everyone the story. They thought I was drunk, no one believed me. I was very frustrated and became furious. I stormed out of the house and slammed the door behind with *Jakaki* still on my shoulder. I laid him down in the back of his car and drove him to his house back in the city.

Then I went home and took a seat and tried to analyze what happened earlier that night. I couldn't understand it. Would anyone ever believe me? I was sure *Jakaki* wouldn't remember any of this when he became sober. Also there wasn't anyone else there and what occurred that night was too unrealistic for anyone to believe. So, I decided to keep it to myself, until just now when I shared it with you. I will never forget the night I came face to face with *Xtabai*.

⁓

**Faye Zaiden, Grade Six,
Bishop Martin Roman Catholic School**
In the village of Benque Viejo there lives *Xtabai*. She is

unbelievably beautiful during the day. She can fool you and look like a simple village woman walking around. At night *Xtabai* returns to her natural habitat either by a street-side or in the forest where she can lure her victims. Drunk men are her enemies because she thinks they will cheat on other women so she lures them away then she attacks.

One night while I was sleeping, I met with my worst enemy *Xtabai*. She was in my yard when I woke up. The chains of the gate woke me and I started to investigate. I opened the door and there on my balcony sat a woman, crying bitterly. I walked slowly towards my swing chair where she was sitting. One creak on the floor, and I would wake up in heaven. But to my surprise, when we met face to face *Xtabai* said, "Oh, my best friend!" Then she hugged me. She thought I was *La Llorona* because I had on a long night-gown and I always sleep with my long dark hair loose.

We chatted for a long time and at one point she said, "how many drunk men have you killed tonight?" I told her, "a lot." Of course I was lying, but if she thought I was *La Llorona*, I needed to follow her lead. We had a good time together even though she was the *Xtabai*, she had a kind heart. "You make me feel so wonderful," she said. "You too, I guess," I thought. We talked until the break of day and she seemed to fade away in the sunlight. That's when my Mom found me. "Why are you talking to yourself?" she questioned. "But she was right here." I cried, pointing to the swing chair where *Xtabai* had been sitting.

"I thought you were supposed to be over having imaginary friends," my mother responded. Before I could say that *Xtabai* was on the swing with me, she'd disappeared. And until now when the wind blows, I see the *Xtabai* waving to me on the swing set.

Joshua Sanchez, Grade Six

In the village of San Juan Lookout, there lives *Xtabai*. *Xtabai* is a gorgeous woman who lures drunken men into the forest. Once she and her victim are deep in the forest, *Xtabai* transforms. After her transformation is complete, she has a horse head, scales like a snake and a chicken or goat foot. She grows spines too numbering every victim she has killed. She has claws to either rip out guts or decapitate her victims for not treating women fairly.

One night when I was walking home from work I met *Xtabai*. I stood there frozen, then I felt my body moving. I thought to myself, "why am I moving?" It was not me, it was the *Xtabai* controlling me. She lured me into a barn where she threw me against the wall. Next she transformed from that beautiful woman into her true form, that of a monster. I was terrified. Yet I tried not to show emotion. As I looked at her, I noticed she had not unsheathed her claws, but she held me up against the wall. She removed one had from my body and took out her claws. Then I spoke to her, hoping she would understand.

"I have family, please, why kill an innocent young man? What have I done to you?"

That seemed to break the spell and finally she put me down. I could see it in her eyes, she wanted to strike but she could not. She reverted back to her human form, and I saw tears streaming down her face. It was like she too had a family and she let me go.

I sprinted home. I never thought *Xtabai* would let a man go. I am lucky to be alive and for that I am grateful!

↜

**Nikolai Pulido, Grade Seven,
Bishop Martin Roman Catholic School**

In the village of Bullet Tree Falls there lives *Xtabai*. What beauty she has during the day but at night little by little she changes her body from a gorgeous woman to a possessed, nasty, animal-like monster. If you see her it is like you are looking at the devil. She has the face of a dead resurrected horse, almost half of her face is only flesh and bones, the other side is all stitched up. Her scream is as loud as the thunder on a very rainy day. One foot is furry and has the dirtiest horse hoof. Her other foot is also filthy with cuts and stitched skin. The intentions of her looks leads up to no good.

One foggy night while I was fishing with my Uncle I met the Xtabai and my life was never the same. I could not move, not one single muscle. I tried to inform my uncle, but it was absolute failure to even try as no sound was coming out of my mouth. Finally, he heard my whispers. He quietly responded to me to hid under the bench of the boat. I did so while my uncle got his gun. Xtabai saw what he was doing and it just made her more angry and vicious. She screamed as loud as the thunder in the sky. All I did was take a peep from under the bench to see what she was doing. I couldn't believe it, she was… she was actually walking upon the water. Step by step she left trails of blood traveling through the water behind her. With the Xtabai eyes on me and now the warm water in my pants, I was terrified. Then my uncle shot the Xtabai and she just sank in the water as quickly as the blink of an eye. I turned around and slowly rising behind me was none other than the Xtabai. My uncle fainted. I turned on the motor and not even knowing how to drive a boat, I took off across the water. Luckily, we lost Xtabai, but I could still hear her laughter echoing through my ears. Finally, I reached my destination, home. With the horror of encountering Xtabai, I climbed out of the boat. My uncle woke up saying, "What in the world just happened?" I replied, "you don't want to know." What an extreme day!

☞

Tata Duende

Lloyd Lucero, Grade Seven

(With a little help from Kristin Pedemonti, on the last paragraph.)

In the village of San Jose there lives *Tata Duende*. People say he's a dwarf with a dirty beard and ugly rugged clothes that look like rags all stitched together. He can be found in forests. In the stories I've heard he protects the forest. His legend is believed by many Belizean cultures. When he walks he leaves footprints that are backwards. I heard he has a huge sombrero, a hairy face and a beard full of insects and decaying materials.

One night while I was minding my own business a little man peered out of the bush. In a sudden burst of excitement I yelled, "awesome!" Little did I know it was the *Tata Duende*. For a moment I was possessed and I couldn't even blink. One step at a time he came closer to me. Then quickly disappeared into the bush. I decided to look for him out of curiosity. But then I remembered, curiosity killed the cat. However, I did not pay any attention to that myth. I still continued into the bush.

All of a sudden, something touched me. I jumped as high as a kangaroo. I told myself, "be brave. Be brave!" In a little girl's voice, I sang out loud, "la, la, la, la, la, la!" as I walked deeper into the spooky but calm forest. Something said to me, "Lloyd, help me." As I walked further, the faint sound became louder. For a moment I felt something give me the power to see what was not there. A little man showed me horrible men destroying the forest. And then it clicked in my brain, "You're the *Tata Duende*!" He pleaded for my help. But then something strange happened, "Whack!" He chopped off my thumbs. I couldn't believe it. I felt no pain at all. He said to me in a deep voice, "I promise to give your thumbs back if you help me." I just nodded my head.

He lured me to the campsite of the men. I tried all sorts of things to get them to leave, but nothing worked. I shook tree branches. I explained to them the consequences of cutting down too many trees. Nothing. Then *Tata Duende* and I worked together. *Tata Duende* cast a spell on them, and the men fell asleep. I helped carry them from the trees to their truck. When they finally woke up, they were astounded to find themselves out of the campsite. I've never seen someone drive so fast out of the forest. I felt heroic.

In a flash, my thumbs reappeared on my hands. *Tata Duende* showed me the way out from the trees. I learned that he is sometimes a kind, loving and gentle spirit and that he truly cares about protecting the forest.

⤿

Bianca Najarro, Grade Six,
Bishop Martin Roman Catholic School

In the village of San Antonio there lives the ugliest dwarf named *Tata Duende*. He is the magnificent guardian of the animals and trees. He teaches lessons to people. He is also an amazing guitarist. He likes to play tricks on people and sometimes goes into houses to hide your things or rattle the dishes. H also plaits the horse's hair. This ugly dwarf knows where the hidden treasures are. Tradition says to go into the forest and set a mat with a white rooster on it and carve a message onto a tree. Then *Tata Duende* will appear, eat the rooster, read the message and tell you where the treasure is. But be careful because sometimes rather than tell you where the treasure is he will lure you into the bush and you will get lost.

One night I wandered off into the forest where I met a tiny dwarf wearing a tall hat, his feet were backwards. I said to myself, "that is one ugly man." I asked him, "who are you?" He didn't answer. He just glanced at me with a mysterious grin as if he were going to do something bad to me. Suddenly, he placed a spell on me. I tried to run, but couldn't. I stood staring with fear. *Tata Duende* started to walk away from me and so I followed. I was scared and did not want to be alone in the forest. I tried to scream, but I realized the spell made me follow him and it made me silent. And then in a flash of lightening he disappeared. I was lost in the forest. I fainted and fell down. When I woke up I was in my bed. My mother was there. "Wake up," she said gently. I asked what happened. "A man found you in the woods, you had fainted and he brought you home." I was thankful to that man and now I never wander into the forest alone at night. I learned my lesson.

‽

Ruvi Bautista, Grade Six

In the village of Bullet Tree Falls, there lives *Tata Duende*. He is a minute man and guardian of the forest. He is shockingly awkward. His feet are backwards, he is thumbless, and yet is an excellent guitarist. He is three feet tall, about the size of a child and wears a huge brown hat which conceals his face. *Tata Duende* is convinced that since he is thumbless then anyone he meets must also be thumbless and so is accustomed to chop off the thumbs of those who have them.

One night while I was roaming through the forest near to my house, I met *Tata Duende* and my life was never the same. It all began when I was gradually becoming far away from my house. Suddenly, I heard someone playing the guitar far, far away. The notes sounded so beautiful, enchanting, almost perfect that I became totally fascinated and I began following the sound to see who was playing.

Finally I arrived to him, but I could not see the person's face. I was hiding behind a tree for I had a bad feeling. I caught goose bumps and my heart was beating rapidly for no reason. I was sweating and then the playing ceased. And as I peeped around the tree, no one was there. When I turned around a tiny rough hand grabbed mine and I recognized the *Tata Duende*. He surely noticed that I had thumbs, and holding my hand tightly I realized he was about to chop them off with a shiny, sharp, medium-sized machete. As I saw this, I screamed with a high pitch voice of terror and fright. I stared in *Tata Duende*'e eyes; he may have noticed that my eyes were filled with sadness. Unexpectedly he stopped himself and let go of my hand. I didn't run away at that moment as others would have, but bravely spoke to him. I curiously and cautiously asked, "Why do you chop off people's thumbs? Is it simply because you do not have any?" I really didn't expect him to answer, but he did. "I don't know why I do it. My task truly is to guard the forest from those who disrespect it." So I had a brief conversation with him about how there was no need for him to chop off thumbs simply because he did not have any. The conversation concluded when he had a realization, "If I can guard the forest, why not guard the children too, protect them instead of chopping off their thumbs?" I exclaimed, "that's a brilliant idea, I could not have done better myself."

Tata Duende accompanied me all the way to my house as part of his new job. My life was never the same after this because I knew that whenever I was in the forest at night someone would be looking out for me. Although he IS awkward, he can have and share good feelings and deeds from the bottom of his heart. And we can have a positive image of him. This was one of the best experiences of my life.

⟿

Adelita Moh—Teacher, Cayo District

Have you heard of folktales? Roaming spirits? Guardians? Well, in the village of San Antonio there lie stories of a great legend. A tiny rustic man with a huge pointy hat and his feet backwards. He was said to be the guardian of the forest and a trickster toward those who harmed his home.

I was a stubborn child and never believed those stories. Until one evening I learned a lesson to always listen to my mother. I had walked one mile over into the next village to visit a close friend. My mom told me to come back before the sun went to sleep. Unfortunately, I got carried away with the fun, and it was almost nightfall. Immediately I knew I had to bolt towards home. I was alone in the dreadful, pitch-black night and silence roamed around the tiny pathway I crept through. For a minute I thought I heard footsteps from behind me and at another moment, whistling. "I am going insane," I whispered. But in the distance I saw someone's feet, tiny feet, dangling from a branch. Beside him lay a hat, so large and pointed, he appeared almost dangerous. My heart skipped a beat, was it whom I thought it to be? It couldn't be! He must have seen the fear right in my eyes. He smiled at me, tauntingly. I froze and he waved at me. I remembered what my mom told me. I hid my thumbs. I swallowed my fright and waved back at him, each hand with four fingers. He observed me and I gazed at him. Then I felt lost. Abruptly what broke the silence was, "Anna!" Someone called my name, it was my mom. "Now is my chance," I said. And I ran. I dashed toward the voices. Through the bushes, vines and thorns, I felt no pain. I saw a glimpse of him trying to get ahold of me. Luckily, I was able to reach the warm embrace of my mother. The last thing I heard was disappearing laughter, mocking me.

〜

La Llorona

Ekanem Ejike—Teacher, originally from Nigeria, now in Dangriga Belize.

Like Jesus when he walked on the earth, he used parables to send the message home in his teachings. Our ancestors had their "send home" devices too; folktales that would turn a crimson laden child into an angel.

"Be home at 5 pm," Grandma would say, "or else…" In the heart of an eight year old this threat would be completed with, "you will be eating dinner with *La Llorona* tonight."

I'd reply, "Grandma, enough already, do I look like I still have diapers on?" I was determined to come back home as usual when I was good and ready.

I ran off into the evening to meet my friends anxiously waiting for me under the mango tree that stood right outside our home. I must tell you my friends and I were never up to any good, we spent our evenings either provoking old men by taking their walking sticks for a laugh or literally taking candy from babies.

This particular evening we decided to change our routine and off to the river we went, some of us wanted a dip in the cool water but others just wanted a laugh. We were all having so much fun when we realized the sun was taking its leave.

Anna shouted to us, "let's go home girls, it is getting late."

I shouted back, "You girls go, I am not ready yet." All I heard was the thunderous patter of eight-year-old feet. I was alone.

It struck me after a few minutes. I realized I should go after my friends, so I lifted myself onto the bank of the river when I felt a cold shiver run through my body and I could hear the sinister cry of the wind. I felt as if somebody was watching me.

Turning to take flight I spied the white silhouette on the north side of the bank then it disappeared. I looked again and all I saw was a brightly colored kaleidoscope beckoning to me. Curiosity got the better of me as I approached the other side of the bank and what I saw could literally knock the non-existent socks off my feet. The most beautiful collection of dolls any eight-year-old could dream of.

I looked both ways then sat down to play with them, engrossed in the activity. I lost track of time. It took a gentle touch to bring me back. I looked up and there she stood, my eight-year-old nightmare, in an immaculate white dress, and hair that cascaded down her back like a waterfall. A beautiful but sad face, marked with indelible tear stains that looked like tattoos. *La Llorona!* My heart raced, 1,000,000 beats per second. I forgot my name, pores poured out sweat like a geyser. I clutched onto one of those dolls as if my life depended on it and yes if Grandma could see my underwear, it was soaked with urine. I guess I still needed those diapers.

↩

Zyra Itza, Grade Six, Bishop Martin RC School

In the village of Soccutz there lives *La Llorona*. She lives near a river called the Mopan. *La Llorona* usually wears a white dress and has long black hair. She is called the crying woman because she drowned her children.

One night I was playing near the river when unexpectedly I met *La Llorona*. I stared at her from head to toe. It was more terrifying to see *La Llorona* than to hear the many stories about her. Suddenly she was walking towards me and I entered into a state of panic; I didn't know what to do next. I began to scream at her. She answered in a gentle voice, "don't be frightened, you are my daughter. You must come with me."

I was so surprised when she held my hand gently. She was headed to the river just then I remembered what she was going to do to me. She would try to drown me, just has she had drown her own children to spite her husband. I was horrified. I tried to stop her, pulling against her. She carried me into the water and held my head under the water trying to drown me. Frightened and struggling, I heard a loud noise coming down from above. I said to myself, "It must be an angel." I was relieved. It really was an angel.

The angel told *La Llorona*, "this girl, she is not your child, she is an innocent little girl. You must let her go, she does not have to pay for what you did to your children." *La Llorona* let go of my hand and I went running home as fast as I could. I told my parents what had just happened, they were so grateful that I had gotten away from *La Llorona*. They were frightened too and told me I was very lucky the angel appeared. From that day on, I never go to the river at night.

❧

Shanalla Homes, Grade Six

In the village of Camalote there lives *La Llorona*. She is always found beside rivers. She has pale skin, long black hair and wears a long white dress. They say she is always crying by the riverside because she remembers her own children whom she drowned. *La Llorona* is always looking for other children to steal to replace her own.

One night while I was washing the dishes I heard a strange humming coming from beside the river. I told my mom that I was going to see what the noise was. By the time I arrived at the riverside, I heard some rustling in the leaves behind me. I was terrified. So I began to run faster and faster, at that moment I felt a strong urge to get out of the forest. When I turned around,

BLAM! There was the horrifying *La Llorona* staring at me. I wanted to close my eyes, but couldn't. She was glaring at me, face to face. *La Llorona* was so close, she was breathing right in my face. Her breath smelled like rotten eggs and garlic. It seemed she had not been clean for a long while. Her long white dress was all damp, covered with mud and blood.

I wanted to scream for help, but I was paralyzed. I couldn't move. I couldn't do anything; it felt as if she had possessed me with her evil, blood-red eyes. I noticed her nails were dirty, long and caked with blood. I closed my eyes and when I opened them she wasn't there. When I looked again, I saw her walking much deeper into the forest. She stopped for a while, as though she was looking back at me to follow her. I didn't of course and then she disappeared into the forest.

I ran home and explained to my mom what had happened. She told me it was nothing and to go back to sleep. She didn't believe me. When I went to sleep I heard the same humming sound again. I said to myself, "*La Llorona* is following me." My heart was pumping so fast I thought I might have a heart attack. I couldn't sleep because of that horrifying crying and the tapping on my window. I got up and told my mom about the crying and tapping, she told me to go back to sleep, that it was just my imagination playing tricks on me. She still did not believe me, but I know what happened, I was there!

I was still afraid of *La Llorona* of course! I couldn't get my mind off of her, she was stuck in my head like glue to paper. I will never forget my encounter with her. I ask you to believe someone when they tell you something has happened, please. And no matter how old you are, obey your parents and DO NOT go to the river at night!

‿

Note: These stories were written during workshop sessions over two or three days. Imagine what could be accomplished if this unit were utilized throughout several weeks, building upon the lesson plans.

The possibilities are endless. Knowing what happens in two days with these students, imagine what you could do if you were working with them every week.

Appendix A: Strong Word Choices

The following word choice selections are suggestions and are not intended to replace a teacher's or a student's own creativity.

Beautiful—comely, attractive, becoming, graceful, charming, engaging, captivating, handsome, bonny, winsome, radiant

Big—large, huge, enormous, gigantic, gargantuan, giant, immense, great, whopping, extensive, massive

Eat—nibble, crunch, gobble, wolf, munch, chomp, devour, gorge, swallow, gnaw, chew, bite, snack

Good—pleasant, well-behaved, excellent, gracious, phenomenal, extraordinary, unique, fantastic, awesome, super, superior, fabulous, wonderful, amazing, exceptional

Happy—tickled, elated, thrilled, lighthearted, delighted, ecstatic, blissful, jovial, overjoyed, jubilant

Laugh—chortle, chuckle, grin, guffaw, crow, titter, cackle, hoot, giggle, snicker

Look—peer, gaze, peek, stare, glance, peep, glimpse, notice

Nice—pleasant, kind, polite, satisfying, enjoyable, pleasing, pleasurable, lovely, amusing, cheery

Sad—pitiable, downhearted, woebegone, forlorn, dispirited, miserable, wretched, dejected, disheartened, depressed

Said—whispered, cried, screamed, hollered, shrieked, bellowed, believed, wept, howled, wailed, blubbered, shouted, exclaimed, called, yelled, screeched

Small—tiny, miniature, teeny, little, microscopic, petite, undersized, minute, diminutive

Walk—swagger, saunter, shuffle, meander, amble, stroll

Went—traveled, meandered, scurried, trotted, hurried, scuttled, rushed, darted, dashed, bustled, crept, crawled, edged, strolled, roamed, wandered, ambled, scampered

A suitable thesaurus is always recommended, but here's an online resource you may want to make use of:

http://www.slideshare.net/mfarrer/plcword-choice

> ➤ With good word choice, the writer creates a mental picture for the reader by using words that are specific and accurate.

> ➤ The writer uses strong action verbs whenever possible to show the reader what is happening rather than tell the reader.

> ➤ The adjectives are as descriptive as possible. The nouns are specific, not general.

> ➤ Striking words and phrases catch the reader's eye, but the language is natural and not overdone.

> ➤ Strong verbs show instead of tell.
>   ▷ The jaguar ate the deer.
>   ▷ The jaguar devoured the deer.

> ➤ Single verbs show better than verb/adverb combinations.
>   ▷ He uses time wisely when writing essays.
>   ▷ He maximizes time when writing essays.

> ➤ Be verbs (am, is, are, was, were, be, being, been) suck the life out of your writing!
>   ▷ He was hugged by the woman with the Free Hugs sign.
>   ▷ The woman with the Free Hugs sign hugged him.

> ➤ Have/has/had combined with a noun encourage readers to wedge their head in a vice.
>   ▷ Example: I had an argument with the referee.
>   ▷ I argued with the referee

Appendix B: Activities and Alphabetical Book Connections.

Activities and book suggestions for every letter of the alphabet.

Find the Letter of the Week: Each week as you focus on another letter or group of sounds, ask the children to identify objects that start with that letter or sound. In your classroom, you can use items such as books or charts. You can bring items that you might have at home: a map of the world (to find countries), magazines, or free posters from the Tourism Board (perhaps featuring wildlife of plants or places to visit). You can also look at items around the school compound—different types of trees, for example.

Alphabet Game: Clap your hands and slap your thighs in time as a group. Have each child, in turn, say a word that starts with the letter or sound you are focusing on that week as the group claps and slaps. If the child cannot think of a word within three clap-slap sets, the next child takes a turn. Continue for as long as it is fun for the group—perhaps five minutes.

Demonstration of the game. It is fun, it gets the children thinking, talking and also moving!

Alphabet Brainstorm Letter Lists

For each letter of the alphabet featured each week, ask the children to help you make a list of as many animals, foods or jobs that start with the featured letter. For example, if the letter is *A*, ask for help creating a list of animals beginning with *A*: ant, aardvark, antelope, and anteater. If the letter is *B*, ask the children to name foods that start with *B* such as bananas, burritos, buns, and beans. If the letter is *C* ask for jobs that start with *C*: cook, construction, cashier, cookie baker, and computer technician.

There is an awesome book list available from the Association of Library Service to Children at the following link:

http://www.ala.org/alsc/awardsgrants/notalists/ncb

The Letter *A*

Anansi the spider.

Make a list of *A* words on the board: Ant, ape, apple, etc.

Book connection: *Anansi and the Talking Melon* by Eric Kimmel; use this book to talk about *Anansi*, his name begins with an *A*.

Writing Activity: An Awesome or Awful Day: Ask the students to tell you about an awesome day; a day when everything went well. Then, ask about an awful day—when things went wrong. OR, connect to *Anansi* and ask the students to think of another trick they can play. Have them write about it.

The Letter *B*

Blow bubbles and ask the children to pop the bubbles. The only catch is, while they pop a bubble they need to shout out a word that starts with the letter *B*.

Book Connection: *The Baby Bee Bee Bird* by Diane Redfield Massie in which the little bird keeps the animals at the zoo awake all night long!

Book activity: Talk about animals that start with the letter *B*, talk with the children about their ideas for convincing the baby bird to sleep at night. For very early readers, *Bark George* by Jules Feiffer.

The Letter *C*

Ask the children to help you make a list of animals that start with the letter *C*.

Activity: Announce that *C* is for clapping. Play a hand-clapping game. Pair the children and ask them to play "patty-cake" with each other. Each time they clap hands, they need to say a word that starts with the letter *C*.

Book Connection: *Curious George* books. Read one of the stories and ask the children to talk about being curious. What does the word curious mean? Does being curious get George into trouble? Why might it be good to be curious? Example, curiosity might help to create new inventions. George always learns something in the story, he tries new things because he is curious!

The Letter *D*

Book Connection: Easy Reader Dora and Diego Books such as *Diego Saves the Butterflies* or *Diego Saves the Tree Frogs*. Many of the books in this series are about environmental themes, so you can incorporate lessons about protecting the environment. I talk about the ways Diego saves the butterflies. Why is it important to protect the environment? Why is it important to keep the earth clean? How can children help? Ask the children to tell you how they can help protect the environment. As an extra activity, your class can clean the school compound, and the area around your school too.

Activity: Dance! Play some music and Move!

The Letter *E*

Earth, Environment, and Elephants!

Write *E* words on the board, ask the class to give you *E* words to create the list.

Book connections: *Just a Little Bit* by Ann Tompert, all about cooperation between an elephant and other animals who try to make a seesaw work. How do things work out better when we help each other?

Talk about cooperation. Ask the children how they might help each other. Ask them to tell you two things they can do to help each other in the classroom, perhaps you can put the children into groups and ask them to talk about how they can cooperate with each other to get something done.

See the letter *D* for more ideas about the Earth and the Environment … also see the page on Earth Day at the end of this manual. *Earth Tales* by Margaret Read MacDonald is a collection of tales all about helping the Earth.

The Letter *F*

Ask the children to name animals that start with the letter *F*.

Activity: Friends and Family Flowers: Ask the children to bring in a photo of themselves, or draw a picture of themselves, which will become the center of the flower. Then draw pictures of their friends and family on the petals of the flower.

Family Stories: Ask the children to talk to their parents and grandparents about their childhoods and how life was different "back then." Then ask the children to share those stories in class.

Favorite Foods: Ask the children to bring in their favorite food to share with classmates.

Book Connection: Read the *Rainbow Fish* by Marcus Pfister, discuss kindness with the children. Ask them what kind things they can do for each other.

The Letter *G*

Book Connection: *Three Billy Goats Gruff* Find a version of this story and play with it, ask the children to act it out.

Culture Connection: In Belize, this meant *Garifuna*. We celebrated Garifuna Settlement Day with stories or dances or food. Elsewhere, I recommend selecting a sports or historical figure whose name begins with *G*.

Activity: Good. Ask the children to tell you about something good they have done.

The Letter *H*

Happy, Home and Hands

Activity: Draw happy faces and ask the children to talk about what makes them happy. They can write down what makes them happy too!

Discussion: Ask the children to talk about their homes, what makes a house a home? Share thoughts about how love and caring make a house a home no matter how big or old the house is! Talk about animal homes; what do fish call home? What is a baboon home? A manatee home?

Book Connection: *A House for Hermit Crab* by Eric Carle; the children can re-create their own homes in crafts and write about how they would decorate to show their personality. What would they wish for in their home?

Handprint Art: Paint each child's hand and have them make a handprint on paper. They can write what makes them special!

The Letter *I*

Imagine That: Ask the children to draw pictures of an imaginary friend. They can also talk to you about their imaginary friend; what do they like about their imaginary friend, what games does their imaginary friend like to play? Where do they like to go? What is their imaginary friend's favorite food?

Book Connection: If stories: *If You Give a Mouse a Cookie* by Laura Numeroff A mouse eats a cookie, and then an amazing chain of events unfolds. Give each student a large piece of paper, fold it in half at least twice to create eight or more panels on which the children can draw their own If story.

The Letter *J*

Jumping for Joy: Ask the children what brings them joy. Ask them to write down at least one thing that brings them joy, for example: visiting grandma, going to school, eating tacos, etc.

Book Connection: Jungle theme. *Oh No!* by Candace Fleming. Good for participation.

The Letter *K*

Kindhearted activities: Ask the children to talk about being kind. Encourage them to do kind things for each other every day. Make a *Keys to Kindness* bulletin board. You might look up *Child Keys Bulletin Board* on the Internet and print out the one you like. Every time a child does something kind, write it on one of the keys and hang it on the board, see how quickly the board fills!

Book Connection: Share one of your favorite stories about being kind. I love Dr. Seuss's book, *Horton Hatches an Egg*, though it may be too long for your younger students.

The Letter *L*

Light up your classroom with Christmas twinkly lights. If you have a set, bring it in and use it in a classroom display.

Animals that start with the Letter *L*. Make a list: Lion, leech, lizard, leopard…!

Book: *The Jolly Postman* by Chris Van Allsburg

Activity: Write letters to each other: Help the children "write" (if children are too young to do their own writing, you will need to help them) very short letters to each other about what they like about each other. Designate a box in the room with a slot cut into the top and have the children "mail" their letters to each other in the box. At the end of the week, distribute the letters to the children with a short cover letter to their parents asking them to read the letters to their child. These letters can be as short as one sentence. On a small sheet of paper write: "I like _____ (name of student) because _____." For young children, ask each child what they like about the chosen fellow student and write that in the blank for them. It makes the children feel good to share positive thoughts about each other.

The Letter *M*

Manatees.

Book: *I am a Manatee* by John Lithgow

Activity: Talk about the importance of preserving manatee habitat in Belize.

The Letter *N*

Numbers: Count things in and around the school, number of windows, chairs, desks, doors, students, steps, etc.

Book Connection: Any story in which numbers are featured or *Uno's Garden* by Graeme Base, which is also an environmental story.

The Letter *O*

The ocean, talk about the ocean. Eat oranges! Color with the color orange.

Name things that begin with the letter *O*.

Book Connection: *The Rainbow Fish*, focus on talking about ocean life in the story.

Art Connection: Draw an ocean scene. Tell a story about an ocean creature.

Movement activity: Obstacle. Set up an obstacle course for children to climb on, over, off and out. This can be as simple as putting a few items on the floor for the children to walk over, and then go out the classroom door and back into the room.

The Letter *P*

Pigs! Share one of your favorite stories about pigs. I love *Olivia*!

Or you could use Mo Willems Piggie and Elephant books. *Look, We're in a Book*, or *I Love My New Toy* are both excellent!

Activity: Pretend! Ask the children to pretend to be pigs or other farm animals. Walk like the animal, make the sound of the animals.

The Letter *Q*

Quiet and Quilts.

Book Connection: *The Very Quiet Cricket* by Eric Carle.

Quilt Art: Ask each child to draw a picture of something they love. Punch holes in the four corners, tie a string to each of the four corners of each picture linking them together as a quilt and hang on the wall.

Movement: Ask the children to walk around the classroom quietly and quickly.

The Letter *R*

Name animals that start with the letter *R*.

Sing *Row, Row, Row Your Boat*

Rainbow: Draw a picture of a rainbow.

Book Connection: *The Rainbow Fish*, talk about how the Rainbow Fish made friends. Make a rainbow fish.

Art: Do crayon rubbings on found objects like leaves, coins, or small objects placed under a piece of notebook paper, then use a crayon to rub on the paper over the object. Use the color red. Draw rainbows!

The Letter *S*

Name foods that start with the letter *S*.

Super Stars: Use a star template and ask the children to write or say words describing themselves. Help them write the words onto their Stars.

Book Connection: *More Spaghetti I Say* by Rita Golden Gelman. Talk about favorite foods.

The Letter *T*

Sing *Twinkle Twinkle Little Star*.

Book Connection: Tales! Share a Folktale. For very young children I like to share *The Three Little Pigs* or *The Three Little Fish and the Big Bad Shark* by Ken Geist.

The Letter *U*

Make umbrella art and do an umbrella writing activity. Ask children to draw a design of some of their favorite things on the umbrella. Hang the umbrella drawings upside down from a string across the room or on the wall.

Book Connection: *Uno's Garden* by Graeme Base. If you are repeating this excellent book, read it this time focusing on the environment in the story and how all the people changed the environment when they moved in.

The Letter *V*

Name vegetables.

Use a balloon and play volleyball with each other by batting the balloon around the classroom.

Book Connection: *The Very Hungry Caterpillar* by Eric Carle. Read this book to the children. Then read it again and ask the children to name Belizean foods for the caterpillar to eat. Draw a picture of the caterpillar eating Belizean foods.

The Letter *W*

Name foods and animals that start with the letter *W*.

Whales: Search the Internet for whale songs and share their music.

Movement: Sing "Wiggle You Waggles Away" and "Shake My Sillies Out" while the students move to the tunes.

Book Connection: *The Whale's Song* by Dyan Sheldon or any book that talks about the world.

Using a map of the world, talk about places in the world the children might want to visit, or where their ancestors came from.

Wonderful World: share ideas of how to make the world a better place to live.

The Letter *X*

Hide a small treasure in your classroom, maybe a new pencil, or a crayon, or a small notebook, or a candy. Draw a map of the classroom, with an *X* to mark the spot where the treasure is hidden. Have the children hunt for the treasure.

Book Connection: *Fox in Sox* by Dr. Seuss.

The Letter *Y*

Have the children tell YOU what they love about you.

Yellow day, ask the children to wear something yellow. Yodel, sing and yodel! It is fun.

Book Connection: Something with the word YOU in the title, perhaps *Are You My Mother?* By Dr. Seuss.

The Letter *Z*

Write the letter *Z* on the board and the word *zoo*. And zero and zipper.

Name animals at the zoo,

Book Connections: *If I Ran the Zoo* by Dr. Seuss. Ask the children to talk and write about what they would do if they managed the zoo! Celebrate with the book, *Animalia* by Graeme Base, and the amazing illustrations!

↶

The books included in this activity were collected by Literacy Outreach Belize and donated to schools in Belize. The manual was shared with staff so they could use the books presented in several ways.

Appendix C: Using Story to Discuss Bullying

Based on "The Lion and the Wise Old Rabbit," a Panchatantra story from India.[6]

Target Audience: Primary School, but it can be adapted for all ages up through adult and used in teacher training sessions.

Note: You may adapt the following plan however you see fit for use with students, teachers, or parents. The following is a template I have created and used with positive outcomes.

Lesson Plan:

Define: First talk about bullying. Ask students to describe what they think it is and what a bully does.

Story Summary with Lesson Script Incorporated:

Lion is big and tough and bad. He is strong and spends most of his time admiring his muscles and bullying the other animals. He mistreats everyone.

Ask students to expand on the story. Ask the children to name an animal that lives in the jungle. Accept whatever answer they give, if it's not a jungle animal, just say that it could be visiting. It helps encourage participation if you accept every suggestion given.

Ask how Lion bullied that animal. Or provide an example of a bullying action. For example: "Lion loved to pull the monkeys right out of the trees by their long tails and then hit them for no reason." Continue with three or four other examples of bullying by asking the students to tell you other jungle animals and then how Lion bullied them.

---

6. Heather Forest, *Wisdom Tales from Around the World*, August House, 1996.

The story continues: Eventually, the animals became tired of Lion's bad behavior and decided to hold a secret meeting to devise a plan to get him to stop mistreating them. One by one each animal shares an idea. Ask the students to share some of their own ideas of what the animals might do to convince Lion to stop bullying them. In the original Panchatantra story none of the ideas are accepted. All the animals respond, "No, no, that's never going to work." (Invite the students to repeat this refrain.)

Rabbit, the smallest and oldest of the animals presents her idea. (I usually whisper this behind my hand so the idea is not really heard, adds humor.) The animals decide it's the best idea and Rabbit should carry it out.

Rabbit finds Lion and tells him there's another Lion in the jungle even bigger, stronger and more ferocious that he is. Lion wants to see it. Rabbit takes Lion to the well (and points down into the well) telling Lion, the other Lion is, "down there." Lion though big and tough and strong is not smart. He sees his reflection, but not realizing it's himself, he becomes angry at what he thinks is indeed another lion. He shouts. (Children become the echo, making angry "Lion" faces and showing their "claws." Children repeat each following line as Lion's echo)

Become Lion, show your claws and make a mean face and loudly say:

> Hey You! (children repeat after you)
> Who do you think you are? (children repeat)
> I'm King of the Jungle. (children repeat)
> No, you're not! (children repeat)
> Yes, I am! (children repeat)
> Nu-uh! (children repeat)
> Uh, huh! (children repeat)
> ROAR!!!! (children repeat)

Lion becomes so angry at what he thinks is another lion in the well that he jumps down to fight him. When he lands at the bottom of the well he realizes he's been tricked. Rabbit is very pleased with herself. Rabbit enjoys laughing at Lion and telling him there's no way out.

Rabbit claps her hands, rubs them together and walks away saying, "good riddance," leaving Lion in the well.

↪

This is the original ending to the story which was part of a group of teaching tales called the Panchatantra. "What comes around goes around." It is a powerful story to use to speak about bullying and the consequences of our actions.

Talk about the original ending of the story: Is it satisfactory? What might happen now? Is it the most effective solution to the problem?

If the students do not make the connection about perpetuating the cycle of violence, you might want to bring this into the discussion.

Together with the students re-create a more satisfactory ending, one that shows compassion to Lion as well as teaches him a lesson and ends the cycle of bullying. Often bullies are not aware how much their behavior hurts or affects others. This is a great gateway to discussion of bullying and its effects.

Discussion: Let's talk about the story.

> Who are the Main Characters? Lion, Rabbit.
> What is the setting? (where the story took place) Jungle.
> Please summarize the plot (what happened).
> Now ask critical thinking questions.
> If Lion is left in the well what will happen to him?
> What is the deeper message of this current ending?
> The current ending basically says if someone hurts you, hurt them back. What do you think about this way of resolving problems?
> Do you think Lion understands his own behavior?
> Does he realize how he makes the others feel?
> How do the other animals feel about Lion's

behavior?

▸   Why do you think Lion acts the way he does?

Children often come up with great details in this section, they often invent his *backstory*. Maybe he had no parents. Maybe he never went to school. Maybe other animals were mean to him. No one is born "bad." Something usually has happened to create these negative behaviors. As the saying goes, "hurt people, hurt people." Often they feel frustrated or excluded. Let's work together to promote inclusion and also help the bullies among us to change their behavior. Bullying is a cycle, and it can be broken. Many bullying lesson plans only focus on the "negative" of the bully.

Let's work together to retell the ending of the story. There are three tasks.

1.   How can we help Lion learn that his behavior is not good? (And show him compassion?)
2.   How can we break the cycle of bullying?
3.   How we can use his physical strength for something positive. In the story, Lion used his great physical strength for negative, how can we turn that around to something positive? Everyone has some sort of strength.

Take suggestions from the students about what the animals can do to help Lion learn that his behavior, his actions hurt them. Example, they can tell him how they feel when he hurts them.

What can the animals do to teach Lion a Lesson so he will change his behavior? You have a choice. You can continue the story with Lion in the well as the story was told to you. On the other hand, you can go farther back in the story and choose another idea/plan to teach him a lesson. What other strategy could the animals use to help Lion change his behavior? Remember to try to use his physical strength as something positive.

Example: Some students chose to have a big tree fall across the path to the water hole. They could not move the tree without Lion's help. All the animals worked together to move the tree. Lion felt included, and he felt good helping.

On a chalk board, whiteboard, smart board or large tablet take notes of all their suggestions. Have the class provide constructive feedback for answers given:

> ➤ Did the idea make sense?
> ➤ Did it show compassion to Lion?
> ➤ Did it teach him a lesson?
> ➤ Did the other animals have a chance to express how they felt?
> ➤ Does the new ending break the cycle of bullying?
> ➤ Did it use his physical strength as a positive?
> ➤ Did it in anyway include him?

After you decide you have created a satisfactory new ending, serve as a guide and choose students to act out the new ending together. Or retell the new ending yourself.

Note: You can do this lesson as an entire class together, or you can break the class into smaller groups of about five children. The students work together to create their new ending and then each group presents to the class; this works for grades four and up.

Wrap-up:

Discuss if the new ending meets all three tasks/goals. Remind that stories have much to teach us and are valuable in helping us behave more mindfully.

Afterword

STOP: Think. Ask. Listen. Learn.

If you decide to do a project, whether it be replicating this one or pursuing one of your own, I ask you to please, stop, think, ask, listen and learn. We all have amazing ideas, we all have good intentions. However, our ideas or projects are not always what is needed. I witnessed many people and organizations with the best of intentions who did not ask the people they intended to serve what was really needed or wanted. Often as soon as the person who created the program left, their project fell apart because the people on-site were not one hundred percent invested in it.

Take the time to:

Stop and Think. Is what you are offering truly needed? Are you helping or harming? Is your project utilizing local talent? Are you collaborating with local organizations? Are you replicating something that is already in place? Are you utilizing local resources? Are the materials you suggest using readily available?

Ask. Ask questions. Check to see if what you envision is what is needed and wanted. Ask what they need. Ask how your program or project might be modified to fit in with local needs or culture. Ask if locals would like to partner with you. Ask what ideas they already have to address the challenge or issue. Ask if they would make any modifications to what you are doing.

Listen. Listen to their responses. Listen to their requests. Listen to their suggestions for improvement. Listen to your heart.

Learn. Be willing to adapt your ideas and your project to the requests from the local people. Successful projects are created and facilitated by those willing to evolve.

Best wishes to you as you share your passion, connect with others through the cultures and stories that resonate with you. I would love to hear how your project progresses or answer any questions you may have. Please write to me!

- ➤ Email me: info@storytellerkp.com
- ➤ Email me: storytellerkp@gmail.com
- ➤ Friend me on Facebook: Kristin Pedemonti
- ➤ Find me on Twitter: @storytellerkp
- ➤ Follow me on Instagram: storytellerkp
- ➤ Visit my website and share on my blog: www.storytell-erkp.com

Together there is so much we can do.

Above all share from your heart and enjoy the process!

Kindest regards, bubbles of enthusiasm *oOOooOOooo* and Hugs of encouragement,

—*Kristin*

After the Afterword

Serendipity or Paparazzi? When one asks about a light bulb of inspiration going off or how Literacy Outreach Belize all came together, I have to say that it was not just one light bulb. It was so many light bulbs, it was like the paparazzi! Scores of chance meetings (some on crowded buses) were with people who knew a principal or a teacher in another village and convinced me that I should go there next. Some encounters were unplanned visits to institutions such as the Main Library Branch in Belize City one January afternoon. Some were connections made by host families or local officials. Every one lead to another teaching opportunity.

That Belize City Library visit opened the door to training Librarians from twenty of the thirty-two country libraries in the Country. Training those librarians led to touring with the National Library Service to fourteen far-flung rain forest villages that were inaccessible to the usual gringa. Partnering with the Belize National Teacher's Union to promote the Teacher Training Workshops and offering workshops in several regions of Belize lead to workshops for current teachers and those studying to become teachers at the University of Belize, St. John's College, Sacred Heart Junior College, and Ecumenical College.

College work led to touring twenty villages in the northern part of Orange Walk District. Through a chance meeting with businessman Rosendo Urbina, I found funding for one month. Through last-minute donations from elementary schools, a high school senior, Allison Rotteveel's volunteer project was realized. Showing up by chance at a Rotary Club meeting when the featured speaker had just canceled resulted in my being asked if I would like to present that very day. At one point, I was even funded through a chance meeting on dating website *Plenty of Fish*, no strings attached. Somehow, when a connection was needed, it appeared.

When you have a passion and you take the first step in faith, the pieces come together. At least they did for me. Trust in your passion. Listen to your heart. Take that first step. Like me, you may be amazed at what unfolds for you.

About the Author

Award winning, cause-focused Storyteller, Kristin Pedemonti, is a TED Talks talent search finalist, and now is a storytelling consultant at the World Bank. In 2005, she sold her home and possessions to create and then facilitate Literacy Outreach Belize. She has conducted programs for thirty-three thousand youth and trained eight hundred teachers on the use cultural stories in the classroom. This book is the culmination of that project. Having performed live storytelling In Kenya, Romania, Italy, Columbia, and Ireland, Kristin was the first American storyteller invited to present at the Kanoon International Storytelling Festival in Iran, February 2015. Watch a video here: https://www.youtube.com/watch?v=bTNFIAAZFvo